"Heartfelt and fascinating." —*BOOKLIST*

"Vikki Warner's memoir is wry, smart, personal, and pretty damn punk rock in its story about life as a semi-together feminist twentysomething trying to balance utopian visions of community, friendship, and romance with the harsh realities of crappy tenants, a dilapidated Victorian, and brutal New England winters."

—**KATE SCHATZ**, author of *Rad Women Worldwide*

"*Tenemental* is an unflinching love letter to a city, a neighborhood, and the notion that *staying* can be a good thing. Cheers to Vikki Warner, whose tenacious and inspiring coming-of-age story gives voice to a new generation of independent women and grown-ass boss ladies."

—**MARGOT KAHN**, coeditor of *This Is the Place: Women Writing About Home*

"Vikki Warner's warm and witty memoir of landladying is a Gothic tale turned inside out. At its center is an old run-down house, but the world *Tenemental* inspires is full of color, life, and that special type of real, earned wisdom that only comes with taking risks and trusting completely in your own young self."

—**KATE BOLICK**, author of *Spinster: Making a Life of One's Own*

"An ode to the messiness of life, *Tenemental* is the incredibly raw, touching, and laugh-out-loud story of a woman figuring out how to get by in the world while doing as little harm to it as possible."

—**EMMA RAMADAN**, co-owner of Riffraff Bookstore

TENEMENTAL

ADVENTURES OF
A RELUCTANT LANDLADY

VIKKI WARNER

FEMINIST PRESS
AT THE CITY UNIVERSITY OF NEW YORK
NEW YORK CITY

Published in 2018 by the Feminist Press
at the City University of New York
The Graduate Center
365 Fifth Avenue, Suite 5406
New York, NY 10016

feministpress.org

First Feminist Press edition 2018

This book was made possible thanks to a grant from New York State Council on the Arts with the support of Governor Andrew M. Cuomo and the New York State Legislature.

First printing June 2018

Cover design and illustration by Amanda McCorkle, colorquarry.com
Text design by Drew Stevens

Library of Congress Cataloging-in-Publication Data is available for this title.

To my parents,
who never take on more house
than they can handle,
and to D. L., who proved
more than willing to.

Contents

Author's Note

I have changed the names of many—but not all—of the people in this book. Some have given express permission for their real names to be used. In some instances, I stepped out of the actual chronology of events, assembling a timeline that would benefit the larger story. I consulted with some of the people who appear here both to check my memory and bring to mind further details. Outside of those caveats, this book is a true account of my experience as I remember it.

Preface

Imagine you own a large house. It's a charming, old place with many rooms and decent-enough bones. Not stately, but attractive in its old-world, banged-up way, and historically significant to its neighborhood. Now imagine that—as in a hazy Stevie Nicks music video dream sequence complete with gauzy fabrics, silver bangles, and skeleton keys—you breathlessly try every door, but you can't gain access to most of its rooms. They remain locked, secret; you stand dejectedly by. You're the mistress of this domain, but you're also the interloper.

This is the life of a landlady.

This is my life.

I have chosen to own a complicated home.

Over many years of gazing at closed doors, I've stopped worrying so much about what might be behind them. In the interest of my mental health, I've categorically stopped trying to fix whatever might be wrong back there. If I catch a whiff of rankness emanating from behind a closed door, I do not obsess over the piles of crusty socks, stale cigarette butts, and elderly pizzas that probably caused it. I just go to my own little cluster of rooms, burn some

Palo Santo, put caulk on something, and *live my own damn life.*

I've worked for years to come to this point of blissful, possibly counterproductive detachedness. I'm countering my natural state in doing so—a default setting that for years had me worrying over every little creak and every little crack. But no matter how diligently I try to disengage, I still occasionally awaken at 4:00 a.m., adrenaline pumping, with the certainty that the house is literally crashing down around me.

Prologue

In August 2004, when I was in my midtwenties, I bought an abused hundred-year-old three-family apartment building in the Federal Hill neighborhood of Providence, Rhode Island—New England's third-largest (and first-freakiest) city. I've lived on the third floor, and rented out the two apartments below, ever since. It's a standard triple-decker, that dime-a-dozen housing paradigm first built to shelter immigrant mill workers, visible everywhere in urban New England, and by the hundreds in my own neighborhood.

Between endless repairs, unruly tenants, a trashed, party-heavy neighborhood described as "troubled" on the local news, break-ins, serial neighborhood house fires, accidents, and just paying the bills, the house has been a needy bitch. And although the two of us are still standing, maintaining our uneasy partnership has been a struggle from the get-go, often hindering my other relationships, and causing me to question the very trajectory of life. Is it all worth it, just to have this big, unwieldy house? Just to stick with this maddening yet adorable friend who is the very definition of high-maintenance? Exactly which of my life goals am I fulfilling by ignoring the mile markers other people use to measure their lives and opting instead to coddle a cranky and battered apartment building in a downtrodden neighborhood of a small postindustrial American city? And *why, WHY* do I find it acceptable to rent apartments to people who smoke crack, or break bathtubs with sledgehammers?

That's right, this story's not just about me and my crumbling, ancient house. It's about me, my crumbling, ancient house, and a host of other disoriented humans stumbling through their third and fourth decades herewith. Starting out as a landlady, I didn't have siblings, a spouse, or kids; *no sweat*, I thought, *who needs such fetters when I have the volatile frisson of living with renters?* As I age, my tenants get younger. As I get more settled in life, they become more erratic. It's all very My First Apartment around here, a dude-centric assemblage of cigarette butts, beer cans, Black Sabbath, and *Rock Band*. Their cumulative comings and goings have shone a light for me into the reaches of the modern young male brain. It's dry kindling in there, and I'm just trying to keep it from sparking up.

I find myself attempting to predict my tenants' next erratic moves, hoping against hope that they're not trashing their apartments, and living in a state of low-simmering paranoia that something may catch fire or explode at their hands. I do not exaggerate when I say that a tenant's late-night burnt toast once brought me to engage in a militaristic sweep of the house.

Over the decade or so since this house has been

in my name, I've filled it with an outlandish array of people (80 percent male) and animals (60 percent feline): punk farmers, herbalists, body piercers, musicians who play metal, punk, country-rock, psych, and folk (or some combination thereof), chefs, bike mechanics, angry straight couples, boisterous gay couples, couch-crashers, geeks, losers, insomniacs, hippies, alcoholics, artists, pit bulls, Dachshunds, Chihuahuas, ferrets, and a bona fide cat parade.

You can smell the reefer a mile away.

One guy has stayed for ten years and counting; another took off unceremoniously a week after his lease was signed. Another destroyed his apartment under the guise of "renovation," then skipped out when he realized he could neither fix it nor pay the rent. Still another tried to have his baby grand piano professionally moved into his second-floor apartment. And a couple of pyrotechnically inclined tenants had a short but fervent stint of lighting fireworks in the driveway right around 3:00 a.m. While this is the most literal instance of combustion on the premises, most of us have endured slower burns of a psychic variety, sometimes setoff by the very people with whom we share space.

Life objective–wise, I haven't set up camp exactly where I thought I would. I'm stuck in an internal tug-of-war that one minute tells me I'm a champ for maintaining a house and treating my tenants well, holding down a fulfilling job, nurturing creative pursuits, and adoring my friends and family; the next minute, that I'm an aging looer with no bluckbuster prospects, no big five- or ten-year plan, no babies growing up fast. I'm happy not clinging too heavily to institutions, but I'm not entirely solid on hanging my hat where I've landed, either. The middle ground is decidedly squishy, as it turns out.

I bought PennHenge (why should only country estates get names?) in the summer of 2004, at just about the most bloated moment of the real estate bubble, and in those days even an insipid fixer-upper built in the Stone Age was almost over my head, financially. Rather than seeing that as a reason to wait, be cautious, save more, I dove in with abandon. It shouldn't have worked. I should have been tossed out in the street with the hordes of foreclosed-upon McMansioners. The only reason I'm still doing the backstroke in this particular pool is because I bought a three-family building. The proverbial envelope of rent money slipped under the door, plus occasional credit overuse, has saved my ass during lean times of frantic money-shuffling.

Driving to work in my rattling stick-shift Toyota in 2007, getting my NPR on, I remember that the news about the economy was starting to sound bad; on subsequent days that news got worse, and then still worse; and then the NPR guys were suddenly referring to something called the Great Recession. "Don't give it a name, you assholes, you'll only make it worse," I demanded of my car radio. Now that I was going to have to dodge not just a diminutively named "downturn," but a massive, looming, capitalized "Recession," my anxiety quickly notched upward. I had a sickening feeling I'd only get by on incredible luck and off-loading valuables on eBay. I was working for a small audiobook publisher, and as my coworkers and I wondered how stable our jobs were, I'd yelp, perhaps a bit dramatically, "Who needs freaking *audiobooks* at a time like this?"

I gritted my teeth and avoided the headlines about plummeting home values. I didn't lose my job—the company I worked for was headquartered in the UK, which perhaps helped to keep a lid on things—but I did watch as a number of houses on my block were boarded up or burned down, and the neighborhood's population decreased to an unnerving low. In the past five years, as the worst financial hangover in modern times has lifted, everybody in Providence has seemed to have a trailblazing business idea— due equally to their own resilience and drive *and* the utter dearth of jobs in Rhode Island, a little epicenter of extreme unemployment during the recession. The city's precipitous nosedive was cut short by this slew of individuals and small businesses doing their own thing just at the moment that "Shop Local" became a bumper sticker.

In some neighborhoods of the city, and prominently in the square mile or so around my house, the past half decade has seen foreclosed or damaged properties being snapped up, fixed up, and resold to real estate corporations or absentee landlords; now, rents are climbing. The sounds of construction bounce between the houses on nearly every street. The long-vacant, goofy, crooked, idiosyncratic little buildings on the streets of the West End—once home to lunch counters, social clubs, and taverns— have given way to their modern equivalents: hipster chicken shacks, cocktail bars, coffee shops, and boutiques. Just about every space is in use again, or on its way there. Well-heeled people drive in from the suburbs to eat and shop in parts of the neighborhood that inspired heavy purse-guarding a few years ago.

Now, I love small businesses; I love good coffee; I love adzuki and oysters and botanical gin! I don't begrudge new business owners their chance to reach for the damn stars. But it's happening so fast, and it's already changing the character of the neighborhood. Where there is success for some (mostly white) people, for others (mostly people of color) the neighborhood is creeping toward untenable cost. I have to make sense of my own possible contribution to the change, whether—having paid too much for my house in 2004—I somehow helped to boost the financial outlook of the block, the street, the neighborhood.

Though the upmarket niceness is closing in around us, Penn Street is still a strange jumble of lawlessness and grime within this illusory bubble, which gives me a counterintuitive little thrill. Some places are insulated against attempts to gussy them up. Those of us owner-occupants who have been here awhile stay quietly in place, taking our trash out on Thursdays and giving the side-eye to abandoned mattresses that stick around a little too long. Though we all make our small improvements, they don't tend to last, and in the meantime more litter and graffiti and broken stuff appears.

Stay nasty, Penn Street, you gem.

I won't make excuses for the landlords of my neighborhood or anywhere else—especially those who don't live in their "investments." Every renter has a nearly implausible story about their shadiest landlord(s) ever. From what I've seen, many of my rental-property-owning colleagues are short-sighted, cheap, greedy, hardened, ruthless corner-cutters—including most of those I rented from before I joined their shadowy ranks. Some landlords own so many buildings they can barely recall them all. Here in Providence, the average landlord is one part blowhard boor, one part petty miser, and one part used-car salesman. Nice people put up with being strong-armed, ignored, ripped off, and cajoled by their landlords. The promise of a really stellar apartment is just about the only thing for which Americans will hold their tongues and take such abuse.

It's no mistake that I'm referring to land "lords" and not "ladies" here. What reasonable single woman would sign up to do this job? Especially when our culture's perception of a landlady (hairnetted, lonely, overreactive, spiteful) is decidedly less flattering than its image of a landlord (prosperous, shrewd, in control, assholery somehow justified as toughness)? The women I know who rent apartments to tenants are fairly young, dangerous with a spreadsheet, and firmly in charge of their homes and lives, so we might want to update the accepted shorthand "generic landlady" image of an angry, broom-wielding old lady.

When I lose myself in overwhelming thoughts about the house, about where it's all going, a guilty urge erupts to the surface: "Go," it whispers.

"Take refuge in a neat, sturdy cape in the nearest upper-middle-class suburb, one with precision-cut lawns, shiny late-model cars, and aggressively ordinary families." But that fantasy is largely based on fear: fear of the disorganization, dirt, and unpredictability of my current situation. Something else drives me to stay here—and it's not just that I may be slightly underwater on the mortgage.

You're soon to learn why this house embodies the framework of every good and bad decision I have ever made. In over a decade of life here, things have gone way right and way wrong, and somehow it's all connected to the bricks and horsehair holding this outfit together. It's solace; it's stagnation; it's the high of love and the grief of watching it fall apart. It's ugly; it's beautiful; it's an anchor; it's freedom.

Put your stuff down, and let me show you around.

Anchor Down

I let him convince me.

His personality was stronger than mine. He spoke with a harsh candor that was by turns hilarious, grating, insightful, and performative.

For five years or so, I'd been sitting back and listening to my artist boyfriend James, appreciating his casually sociopathic worldview and enjoying his unpopular opinions about world conflicts, government conspiracies, rich kids, and bad art. We'd been cohabitating in Boston for a few years, making vague moves toward living in a way we could live with—scratching out a small space to inhabit in a staid city. Accordingly, we'd been wide-eyed bystanders to the ruthlessness of the early 2000s housing bubble in Boston. We watched prices creep up and then skyrocket, and found it chillingly intriguing. The lazy walk home from dinner or the bar often involved stopping to gawk at the listings posted outside the real estate agencies in the neighborhood. Such gawking led, naturally, to flamboyant complaining about the insane prices. $400,000 for a one-bedroom condo in an outlying area? $650,000 for a cute but dilapidated little house in a boring place on the outskirts of the city? Secretly ensconced within the grousing, though, there was deep longing.

Armed with little information other than our own self-perpetuating opinions, we somehow insisted on wanting to buy in. Armed with little money, we wondered how we would ever do it.

"This shit is going so crazy. It's all closed off to regular people. Eventually you won't be able to buy anything unless you're one of these super-rich fucks."

"Totally. It makes me nervous; it's like, if you don't get in now, you *never will!*"

James goofed on me a little for my seriousness, for my love of organization, for my mousy literary disposition. I typically buttoned up while he and most of our friends were getting wild. For a span of time he called me "Sally Blazer, Roving Reporter"— which I took as a compliment, an acknowledgment of my tweediness and tenacity.

At twenty-six, in my third year of working a straightforward but uninspiring job as an editor for a medical publisher, I had a few dollars in the bank—somewhere around $15,000—on a major-for-me salary of about $56,000 a year. I was proud that I'd been able to save, considering all the obligations I'd stuck myself with: grad school tuition, rent, repairs to my broken little Honda, intermittent underemployed boyfriend support. I was paying the bills like a champ. But in so doing I had adopted a somewhat joyless lifestyle, scrimping on time and money, filling every hour with work and school and believing in my own American ambition to *never stop doing stuff.*

I grew up in a trailer park, the child of two humble earners who worked hard, saved peerlessly, moved shrewdly, and still had just enough to get by. I felt a shaky charge when I gazed at my bank statement and saw that fifteenish grand looking back at me. I didn't understand the relative scale of wealth; I thought my little bundle of cash put me into a new echelon, a bump up on the ladder, when in fact the sum total of my nest egg didn't come close to moving the needle for someone with real money, those people who seemed to be everywhere around Boston: the ones who owned the beautiful houses on leafy acres, their BMWs parked on the heated circular drive, or the aloof downtown high-rise condos. At that brief moment in my twenties, stoked by the crude gratification of suddenly having more money than I'd ever seen before, I would have given up all of my punk ideals to double the cash in my savings account. The dot-com bubble had only just burst. This time was all about free-flowing money—the feeling had been that all you had to do was stick your hand into the bubbling wellspring and grab some. The lights had gone out on the economy, but the spending party continued, only getting nastier under cover of darkness. Buying stuff—whether with real or imagined money—was a national balm against recognizing that the economy was soon to puke on its shoes.

I got nervous. I got downright itchy. Would I ever be able to afford not to rent? My coworkers were snapping up ho-hum condos just to get a foothold in this gruesome market, figuring they'd stay a year or three and then cash out, moving up until they had the houses they *really* wanted. Every property was going quick, now-or-never, for the asking price and then some. This was both terrifying and alluring, and in my upwardly mobile stupor, I felt the unmistakable twinge of *wanting in.*

I was living with five roommates—all men—and I was burnt out on dirty dishes, moth infestations, food on fire, and pubes in the shower. James and I wanted to shake off the indignities that our living situation forced upon us; we wanted to slow down and have our own space. I felt a primal need to comb flea markets and salvage warehouses for perfect, incredibly cheap antique doorknobs and mirrors. I had an inexact but appealing vision for it: a sweet, old house with art on every surface, a cat or two, a lot of blankets, a decent stereo.

I didn't have the money to buy anything in Boston, and anyway, I was over it. I'd been there almost five years, and the city had never opened itself up to me. It was expensive and stodgy and nerdy. It felt devoid of opportunity. I had about five friends, whom I loved, but none of them seemed especially happy there either. Being jammed up, in denial of one's own emotions, is the Boston way. Fun is meted out in small doses. I was in danger of getting carried away on that tide, overextending myself every day just to live in the same boring town.

"I mean, New York could be perfect. If I want to be in publishing, that's really where I need to be," I said, on a taking-stock-of-options walk around the neighborhood with James, the dark, old, unaffordable houses of Jamaica Plain looming over us.

"Yeah. For art too. It's so expensive though; we'd have to live in some shithole. I read an article—there's like a rat *epidemic* happening right now."

In a month or two of further conversations, during which we never discussed the future of our own lives together, only the future of our respective careers and individual prospects, we tossed away the idea of moving to New York. Too expensive, too big, too many people, too frenetic, we reasoned. We were both small-town kids at heart, and an unspoken fear had arisen between us: New York would swallow us whole. New York would quickly poke holes in our fragile psyches, and consequently, in our relationship.

"I'm freaked out about not being right near the ocean. And it takes too long to get to the woods from New York."

"Well, whatever, we could get on the train and be in Rhode Island in three hours. Or take the commuter train out to the Hudson Valley."

"True." Silence.

Another option was to move back to Providence, the adorable but horribly mismanaged capital city of our adorable but horribly mismanaged home state of Rhode Island. We were sheepish about "going backward"; we'd be giving up on big-city life so easily, and we were both embarrassed by this seeming lack of ambition. We wanted to be bold, but we stopped short, failing to double down by moving to the very biggest of cities. We might have been giving up just before some huge payoff, but we knew we didn't have the drive to go there and fight the hordes of shrewder, cuter, more confident people.

And so, freaked out, we decided to return to Providence. For all the talk of moving to a place that would bolster our careers, our little capital city was likely to kill them unless we both got infinitely more creative in pursuing freelance work. For now, I would keep and commute to my job just outside Boston, an hour each way from Providence on a good day. On the plus side, the cost of living in Providence was half that of Boston, and a third of what we'd expect to pay in New York. To soothe the sting of backtracking, we dreamed up this very jet-setting idea that Providence was just a "base of operations," from which we would make frequent work-related trips to faraway locales where our editorial or art services, respectively, were desperately needed.

Both James and I had spent a lot of time in Providence as teenagers, going to punk, indie rock, and hardcore shows at Club Baby Head, eating truckloads of falafel in our Army/Navy surplus fashions, and buying records at Tom's Tracks. We'd lived there for one year together, before Boston, in a moldering apartment on the East Side where we had to kick out a squad of sleepy art students with yeast infections (there were tubes of Monistat all over the apartment) in order to move in. "No, seriously, we rented this place, and it's June 1, and you need to leave *today*." It's not clear why we needed to perform the extrication ourselves, without help from our beleaguered landlord; in hindsight, this may have been my first taste of the bewildering landlord archetype.

All told, Providence had been decent to us, and we tried to recognize the pros and cons before committing to go back. It was a fun town, we had friends to hang with, the ocean was close enough to sniff in the air, and there was a thriving art and music community for us to wedge ourselves into—one with infinitely more life in it than the anemic scene in Boston.

The watershed moment came innocently enough. James casually laid it on me.

"I don't wanna just live in another shitty apartment. I'm sick of renting." And later, the wheels turning: "You should buy a triple-decker—the rents would cover the mortgage and you'd live there for basically free."

I sputtered. I don't remember what I said in reply, such was my shock at his statement, both the concept itself and that his suggestion was made under the category of "you" and not "we." But he'd struck the match. It had begun.

Just for laughs, and thinking it would surely go nowhere, I called a couple of mortgage brokers. I started trolling Rhode Island real estate listings, my heart pounding, my eyes locked down on rows of search results. In a story that has since become a classic of pre–Great Recession let-the-good-times-roll abandon, I was instantly preapproved to borrow $300,000 after giving up a little personal information, some W-2s, and a couple of paystubs. I had good but very limited credit, being that I was young and had never made a major purchase—I wasn't even paying back my student loans yet. Still, it was stupidly easy; I ignored the fine print and scrawled my signature, mostly unsure of what I was signing up for.

In an instant, I was on the carnival ride, with the operator asleep at the controls. I couldn't get off this thing if I wanted to. If I said "I want money," money would be passed to me from some shadowy entity. Strange as it seemed, everyone was doing it, so why not me? The system *obviously* worked—nearly every damn homeowner in America had used it, for everything from bungalows to brownstones. Who cared where, specifically, the money was coming from?

Thankfully, I had the foresight (and parental coaching) to decline an adjustable-rate loan, but such loans were repeatedly offered to me, along with several enticing no-money-down, no-income-verification options. The now-infamous "predatory lenders" smelled my fresh blood, but in a rare moment of good sense I spurned them and planned on an old-fashioned thirty-year fixed rate. Thirty years! James and I laughed at the absurdity of signing up for anything on that kind of timeframe, which contributed to our distinct feeling that this wasn't actually real. We thought it was *hilarious* that I'd be fifty-seven by the time the house was paid for. We'd picture me at fifty-seven (although probably the woman we were picturing was more like eighty-seven), in a shabby little apartment, the place unchanged in thirty years, the shades drawn, the curtains eaten by moths, the walls crumbling, the 2004-era Ikea furniture having been mended countless times. James never mentioned where he thought *he'd* end up, but clearly he was not to be counted in this scenario. So why was I about to buy a house for *us* to live in, when *he* could cut out at any time, and when he wasn't interested in talking about *us* in the future tense? And when I wasn't sure what I wanted, either?

Despite these moments of panic about the future, I spent hours online, parsing and reparsing more listings, funneling my nervous energy into a deepening real estate obsession. I was in it now, riding hard the impossible fantasy of finding the perfect house in the perfect neighborhood at the perfect price. I was hurtling toward something unknown, and even though nothing was yet decided upon, and no real obligations yet created, it felt inevitable. The recurring theme was that if I did not buy a house *right now,* I would *never* be able to afford one. Because prices were just going to keep climbing—FOREVER.*

Ever the haven for the misunderstood and the contrary, Providence has been attracting oddballs since 1636, when it was established by one Roger Williams, a Puritan minister who left England, and was subsequently banished from the Massachusetts Bay Colony, for espousing freedom of religion. Avoiding deportation to prison in England, forced out of a Massachusetts that had become very hot for a person of his beliefs, Williams moseyed south of its confines, and was offered refuge with the Wampanoag and Narragansett people; the latter eventually sold

*Not what happened.

him the land that became the city, which he named in honor of "God's merciful Providence," deeming it "a shelter for persons distressed for conscience."

By most accounts, Williams is portrayed as a fair and respectful man; he opposed slavery, devised the concept of separation of church and state, and enjoyed a long relationship of mutual trust with the Wampanoag and Narragansett tribes. As colonial figureheads go, Rhode Island's are pretty good. The State House is topped by the Independent Man, a golden statue of a loincloth-garbed, spear-carrying man with an anchor at his feet; he represents our strength as well as our renegade streak, and Rhode Islanders are very into him as an icon.

Providence was an early manufacturing leader in America. The first textile mill in the United States was built just a few miles away in Pawtucket in 1793. Mill complexes quickly popped up all over the state and city; employing generations of factory workers, they cranked out textiles, tools, silverware, and jewelry. Rhode Island calls itself the "birthplace of the industrial revolution," and although that is a messy credit to claim—considering the awful things our country did, and does today, in the name of "industry"—the state claims it proudly.

So this state may have once been on its way to national respectability. But give any set of beliefs or commonalities a few hundred years to stew in the pot of a semi-insular population, and they get twisted. The offspring of the colonial settlers, plus that of later immigrants mainly of English, Portuguese, Italian, French Canadian, and Irish descent, have internalized our founders' rogue spirit and added generations of spin on it, not to mention an ear-curdling accent. It's averaged out to a few basic traits many of us have in common: crankiness, sarcasm, tough talk, the ability to take (and tell) a joke, and lazy yet hostile driving tendencies. It's a hard-charging, pint-sized buoyancy that can't help but be endearing and often infuriating.

There's also a heavy distrust of government at all levels, because if there's one thing we've got, it's corrupt officials. Generations of them, each one building on the air of permissiveness and selfishness that came before. Each official painted in his own beautifully nuanced shade of braggadocio, finding new and creative ways to cheat at "serving" the public. "Distressed for conscience," indeed. Innumerable deals were struck between city government and organized crime when the latter ran the show from the mid-1950s through the 1980s. The patron saint of Providence con men is the late former Providence mayor/twice-convicted felon/fame seeker/all-around blowhard Vincent "Buddy" Cianci, whose very name continues to incite devotion and rage in equal proportions among Providence residents.

My Providence brethren have simply learned to live with the patterns of waste and grift in the city, mostly by devising artful new ways to complain and joke about it in our hardass Yankee way. But we stay here because we really love this place. We even love that it is often openly terrible. New Englanders love punishment.

Providence is a college town, and we've ticked a

box in each category: a vaunted Ivy (Brown University); the best art school, some say, on the continent (Rhode Island School of Design [RISD], a.k.a. RIZ-dee); a culinary/hospitality training ground (Johnson & Wales University, or "JAY-Woo"); a traditional Catholic college with a creepy, blank-faced Friar mascot (Providence College) and a public school serving primarily local students (Rhode Island College). Neighborhoods cater to the differing tastes of each student body with run-down Irish pubs with buzzing Bud Light neon signs for the Catholic school and fancy coffee shops and cafes for Brown and RISD. Most locals have some sort of bone to pick with the universities—they take over the choicest bits of real estate in the city, and—due to their mostly tax-exempt status—occupy them, flowing money back to the city only at their own whim. Students crowd the apartment rental market; they are loud, they are messy, whatever. But without the influx of students that comes every year, and without the people who choose to stay after college, this would be a far less lively city, and a far more broke one.

There is a bit of local lore that says if you drink from a particular fountain in the city, you might leave Providence, but you'll be bound always to return. The only part of this statement that is surprising to me is "you might leave Providence," because most of us native Rhode Islanders are shackled to this place on a permanent basis. Our state's flag carries the very fitting image of an anchor; the same image adorns a popular bumper sticker that reads "I Never Leave Rhode Island."

On a short walk in Providence, you can be alternately buoyed by the beauty of the place and its people, and horrified by the mountains of litter, the boarded-up houses, the threatening tenor of peoples' interactions, the alarming amount of street drugs, and the number of straight-up assholes looking to fight or harass women. A new wave of city leadership has taken over, and things have begun to improve, or at least lurch toward modernity. Following a lengthy line of white guys, two consecutive Latino mayors have started us up the long hill of tightening the city budget, sniffing out corruption, figuring out what to do with abandoned properties, reducing crime, and improving public education and housing. But there's still an Old Guard in this town, and their unblinking refusal to accept change—even when that change is geared toward creating stronger neighborhoods, healthy small businesses, better-educated kids, and new jobs—is bizarre and chilling.

When I made the succession of moves that would bring James and me back to Providence, I did it without an adequate understanding of what I was signing up for, the struggles present in the place where we were planning to make a life, and whether I was up to the task. All of those considerations were happenstance to me back then. I never deeply considered what sort of neighborhood I wanted to be part of. I never pinpointed exactly what I wanted my house to look like or contain. I never nailed down my goals for homeownership or a basic timeline for how long I planned to live in said house. I never read a book about real estate, took a class, or even googled "advice for landlords." I thought all it would take was a modest pile of dollars and a little common sense: the tenants pay the mortgage, I do a bit of upkeep, make nice with everybody, fill the place with secondhand but still-classy furniture, and get to use my own paycheck to buy champagne and tropical vacations. *Right?**

On a one-day romp around some of the most unloved properties of the west side of Providence, I looked at the interiors of exactly three triple-deckers before I saw the house I eventually came to buy. Some of the apartments were laid out in the infamous railroad style, where one walks through the living room to get to the kitchen to get to a bedroom, or some variation thereof. They were old houses, but they had been pathetically renovated over the years to feature acres of particleboard and thin, bedraggled carpeting. Bare wires and naked light bulbs hung down. Sunlight strained to illuminate dusty, junk-filled rooms with blankets over rickety windows. Huge, ancient boilers brooded in decaying basements. These houses were beaten down, stained, *tired*. Perhaps some bit of panic set in then—I saw what I could afford, and it did not inspire excitement or even mild interest. My normally clear head felt muddled; counter to any reasonable instinct, somehow it felt like the only way to put my brainwaves right was to just go on and buy the first decent house I saw.

That means I made a monolithic life decision—

*Not what happened.

one that would factor heavily into my existence for potentially the next thirty years—in the space of a couple of hours, and after seeing practically nothing else to which it could be compared.

Since starting the loan process, I had been subject to financial reality check after reality check, and it was now clear: I had very limited resources. Those bank statements I'd been so proud of now looked comically paltry. I moved on to accepting that no matter how many listings I pored over and how many beautiful, way-out-of-reach houses I ogled, I would end up settling for a house that didn't knock me sideways. This was to be a practical endeavor, I told myself, not an emotional one.

"Besides, you can sell it in a few years if you want to," James noted. As if that would be easy.

Buy High, Sell Never

Upon first viewing, the house on Penn Street was filled with contractors and day laborers of varying degrees of professionalism. A husband-and-wife team was tasked with painting the foundation and the garage doors; a stable of plumbers milled about, occasionally yelling from one part of the house to another; an alarming number of discarded Dunkin' Donuts cups obscured every surface. The current owner, Al—a profane house-flipper in a track suit— was holding court, trying to direct the chaos. There was a huge, old car in the driveway, and a lady with her scruffy little dog told us she was living in the car, *in the driveway,* until she got a place to stay or the house was sold.

Not exactly the kind of staging one sees on HGTV.

The house had just been put on the market. James and I were just about the first to see it, and we did so on the realtor's whim after we flatly rejected the other houses he showed us. It was three floors, built circa 1912, with a basic Victorianish exterior and a few surviving charming details, but it was obvious that the piss had been beaten out of this place over the years. We viewed the aluminum siding, with its slightly icky dual tone (light green on the first floor, white on the top two) with open revulsion, but decided it was not as bad as lowest-of-the-low vinyl siding. The street the house sat on was ugly, but it was very close to downtown. It happened to be a neighborhood cleanup day, and happy, joking kids skewered litter into bags.

Once we got inside, it became clear that the house was in the throes of a brutal renovation. Anything with character was on deck to be ripped out and replaced with cheap, bland, made-to-fail building materials purchased in bulk. We'd stumbled onto an old (though tarnished) gem, with an elegant, winding staircase, high ceilings, wood floors, and marble fireplaces, and it needed to be polished, not hollowed out. As it stood, the house felt like a shell, harshly gutted. So many rooms without a finished surface among them—pipes sticking out of walls and floors, old wallpaper half-removed from bowed plaster walls, a veritable history of linoleum decor in ripped layers upon the floors. We somehow found this refreshing rather than overwhelming, as if it provided the blank canvas on which we could project our personalities.

I was personally offended that a nice, simple old house with history would soon be just another drop-ceilinged, industrial-carpeted craphole in a city already filled with them. Al was "fixing it up," he said, so that it would be trouble-free for a landlord— less to maintain or even think about, wasn't that what I'd want? Who needs crown moldings or old wood floors when they're just going to need upkeep?

"Why bother making it nice," he said, "when you're just going to rent it out to a bunch of slobs?"

But Al played along with my whims, amused at my youthful enthusiasm. Over the next few days, as our discussion continued, he agreed to cease and desist on the popcorn ceiling finish and the wall-to-wall Astroturf, but I'd have to make an offer, and soon, because he needed to get the show on the road. I liked the house and thought I could make it some shade of what I wanted. I didn't love the look of the neighborhood, heavy with graffiti, litter, and concrete, but this was the closest I could get to downtown that was in my price range. I used my favorite mantra, "I'm sure it's fine," to sweep any misgivings under the rug. I felt like a real grown-up boss lady even *talking* about buying a house. The feeling was intoxicating. I minimized the house's many shortcomings, and played up its charm and age in my mind, just to ratchet up my comfort level and make this a doable "project" rather than a dreadful maze of expensive chores.

Al had the house listed at $275,000. Feeling as detached as if I were playing Monopoly, I talked to my real estate agent (henceforth "the Unrealtor"). He believed the house was solid, although he admitted it needed some work. He thought the neighborhood was "on the upswing," and I should "get in now." (I really wasn't into becoming a mogul—I wasn't very interested in appreciation, of the eventual selling price, of building a low-end empire. But explaining my unambitious real estate aspirations to a guy like him, whose money was made by buying and selling buildings, did not compute.)

I settled on offering $250,000, contingent on the immediate cessation of Al's prior renovation plans, and including a note about his consulting me before making any major moves. (This plan would save Al money, because he'd be skipping some major projects—carpeting, windows, interior painting.) He countered with $260,000. I said $255,000. We settled on $257,500. At the end of May 2004, in a haze, I signed the purchase and sales agreement, including a list of repairs and improvements to be made before the closing. The Unrealtor egged me on, latching on to my irrational excitement, practically pushing the pen along the paper. My hand moved accordingly, but my brain was mired, sluggish. I handed over the deposit. James and I high-fived. And we promptly went home to the apartment in Boston and continued to pretend this whole thing wasn't real.

In unguarded moments, I asked myself what the fuck I was doing. I'd just dropped an initial $7,500 deposit, knowing that the options then became (a) buy the house or (b) lose the cash. I'd felt that foreboding hand of fate clamping down on me—the one that told me to just do this and everything would suddenly become clearer—as soon as we started looking in earnest. Coming from Boston, where a similar house would have cost double or more, I thought Providence and this house were a bargain, although I had friends who'd bought there a few years earlier for many thousands less. But again—this had to be the time. I couldn't wait. I'm the kind of slow plodder who completes the task at hand, even if it means my own demise. I wasn't going to back out.

If you live in New York or San Francisco, you snorted some really good cold brew through your nose when you read the purchase price of my house. I know, it seems filthy cheap. It's a big three-family apartment house with a garage, a driveway, and a yard. It's in a centrally located (if not pretty) neighborhood of a hipster college town with really good food. But make no mistake, this was midbubble pricing. Ten years earlier, you could've bought three gorgeous houses on the west side of Providence for $257,500. My mom knew it, and in her no-nonsense tone she said, "Are you nuts? A quarter of a million dollars?" But I was not in the mood for cautionary guidance. I was more interested in paint swatches and antique furniture.

In a certain sense, I bought the house partially to keep it from being ruined by Al's plywood henchmen, and partially because I felt I had to grab at something—the chance would be gone so quickly. To my mind, there was no time to thoughtfully consider all the angles. I liked it, yes, but I also felt a bit desperate in this early 2000s environment of rapturous homebuying. Being told that "it's going to be on the market for a couple of days, at the most," I panicked, and I played along.

The details of the transaction were hazy. There would be a period of renovation, during which Al and his scrappy assembly of uncredentialed workers would put in toilets and stoves and fridges and finish the house more or less to my specifications, which were simple and not much pricier than the plastic and cardboard junk they'd been planning to use. Al never would have agreed to anything expensive, but I had my eye on some low-cost materials that didn't look so janky. Then, after appraisals and inspections and a final, illustrious walk-through, we'd all attend the closing, shake hands, and get this deal signed and my money vaporized. I got that part. But the rest of it—rates and terms and FHA requirements and loan types and points and closing costs—I barely even tried to understand. I dreamily figured it would all work out. (Reminder: I was twenty-six.)

The Unrealtor—a relative of a friend of a friend—was clearly afraid of Al. Federal Hill has a deep, notorious history of Mafia connection—it was for decades the very public base of operations for organized crime in New England. Men were shaken down in the five-and-dime and shot as they tucked into plates of linguine at the lunch counter. Corruption and violence were part of daily life. The Family infiltrated and manipulated local politics, business, and law enforcement until the nineties, when the local boss and twenty of his associates were indicted; a severely weakened mob moved back to Boston. Today, the last bastions are quietly disappearing from Providence, although everybody knows where the leftovers are. Think: less murder, more gambling and money laundering.

Though I highly doubt that Al had a connection to the actual mob, our real estate agent boomed wary of his hard-ass demeanor and old neighborhood accent, so he was overly jocular and obliging toward Al, taking me out of earshot so he could gently coach me not to complain or ask for too much. I had to do most of the talking. Luckily, though Al was vulgar and aggressive in his other business dealings (his cell phone conversations made frequent use of the word *cocksucker*), he was a pushover when faced with a little lady with silly, stupid, delightful ideas about maintaining the style of the house instead of turning it into a soulless dormitory.

I kept my parents apprised of my progress, leaving out some of the sketchier bits. They were supportive enough of my decision to buy the house, but they were clearly baffled by my making this risky move, and by the amount of money I'd be borrowing. They gave me good advice, and they certainly let me follow my misshapen dreams, but didn't say more than they had to. My mom now admits that they secretly hoped I would give up on the whole thing. I can't blame them. They must have asked themselves why I would buy this difficult house in a neighborhood so different from the one I grew up in; why I wasn't getting married and buying a place with my husband; why I couldn't relax and let these big life decisions happen in order; why I was with this guy who wanted me to buy a house but couldn't contribute much actual money to the cause. "Whatever you do, Vik, make sure that house is in *your name only*," my mom warned.

By this time, James and I had been together for six years. He worked part-time at a bookstore and had a one-step-forward-two-steps-back kind of art career. He really pushed himself artistically, but he was disorganized and discouraged. He always seemed to work for dipshits who promised great things, but then couldn't pay. Much of his work consisted of highly detailed, technically flawless pen-and-ink illustrations and screen prints of deranged demons; they were funny and intentionally trashy, in the style of eighties gross-out comics. But they featured too many pimply butts and flaccid dongs to get very far with rarefied art buyers who had cash to burn.

James had no money. In fact, I'd been paying his rent in the Boston place on and off for years (yeah, I know) since he'd been laid off from a dot-com start-up that made fancy websites and promotional videos—a company which seemed to foretell its own demise by naming itself Fiction. Instead of paying into the purchase of the house, we agreed that James would provide labor—he had in the past worked on his brother's roofing crew and done some carpentry—and maybe throw in a few hundred bucks when he had it. He'd also get us a really good deal on roofing and windows, which the house sorely needed, via said brother. Being stubbornly proud of my ability to buy this house pretty much independently, I told him I wasn't worried about being responsible for paying most of the bills. I had faith that I could generate and save money when I needed to. Somewhere in the reaches of my subconscious, I also knew that letting James shirk accountability meant I could continue to claim my status as the long-suffering girlfriend: the one who did all the work, paid for everything, and never complained. I got some mileage out of being the saint in the relationship—the counterweight to his testy and conflicted tendencies.

But buying PennHenge also felt like the first step on my own version of a badass path less traveled. Until this point, I'd dutifully attended college, and then grad school, and I'd had one job or another since I was fifteen. I'd been a saver and a planner, a good girl with punk leanings. I'd never gone on a grand journey of self-discovery; no semester abroad, no epic backpacking trip, not even a cross-country drive. I was firmly planted, all business.

Now I was in my midtwenties, with no inclination toward marriage, and a negative maternal instinct. Buying a big, messy house with broken windows and a decaying foundation seemed, if not the smartest plan, definitely the most apropos thing an Independent Woman could do with her nest egg. And being a landlady? Hell yes. I would be the doyenne of the place. I'd start my own little punk house, and I'd find a ton of like-minded people to share the house's (eventual) charms. Every Sunday, we'd eat a vegan dinner of veggies plucked from our own garden, and we'd drink home brew and laugh by the fire pit, with our little cassette boom box blasting away into the wee hours.

Feeling pleased with my new risk-inclined self, the one who did not slink away from a challenge involving manual labor, I moved onward with the plan. I was actually going to buy this thing. I continued to visit PennHenge once or twice a week while it was being renovated by Al's crew that summer, dropping in unannounced and pointing with feigned authority at things I liked or didn't like. The Unrealtor continued to get mush-mouthed in Al's presence, so Al and I started dealing with each other directly—not the way it's supposed to work—a real cop-out on the Unrealtor's part. Battles with Al were won and lost. He found me a beautiful antique gas stove for the third floor, but he refused to upgrade the bathroom—which had a summer camp vibe, with its flimsy plastic shower stall and tiny sink (plus a door that opened onto the *back of the shower stall* from the next room). Al gave in on the black-and-white kitchen floor tiles I liked, but he wouldn't cave on nicer cabinets. He'd say, "Now didn't that come nice?" when showing off some newly finished detail; when circumstances prevented perfection, he'd squeal, "I hadda do that!" At every turn, we tussled. I knew I could only get so much, and that it would be up to me to fix a lot of things on my own dime later.

Meanwhile, the mortgage proceedings hit a snag, and I was forced again to confront how much money I *didn't* have. I was turned down for an FHA loan, which meant I was required to put up another ten grand, and I couldn't do that and have a single dollar left for moving, painting, and readying the two rental apartments. James—clearly as convinced as I was that there was no turning back—called his older sister, an unerringly patient woman who'd done well for herself and wanted to see the rest of her family equally set up. He talked her into letting me borrow some cash. From her point of view, it probably seemed that James and I would be together for decades, get married, have children (why *else* would we be looking to buy a house together?), so she wanted to help me (us, him) out. Maybe she felt bad for me because she knew James couldn't contribute. Whatever her motivation, with that I sunk further into laughable debt. I shielded my eyes from the amount and trudged on.

On August 4, 2004, the day after my twenty-seventh birthday, I became the official owner of PennHenge. In the days leading up to the closing, I hired a roly-poly, mustachioed home inspector—the cheapest one I could find—who, with his teenage sidekick, reported that the windows were shit (not news), the roof was tragic (indeed), and the plumbing was "Mickey Mouse," contractor parlance for "not installed by professionals." Pluses: the walls were "sturdy as hell" and built by people who "knew what they were doing." He wasn't overly worried about the basement, the walls of which would disintegrate into your hands with a stern poke. There were toxic piles of moldy red-brick dust at regular intervals along the floor. He said this was common in Providence— humidity is unkind to old houses—and looked awful but didn't pose much of a problem. Structurally, that is. "Just don't breathe it in," he advised.

I had hired the cheapest inspector for a reason— so that I could ignore the problems that a more meticulous person would have brought to my attention. Anyway, within an hour or two I had moved on to zealous ramblings about area rugs and paint colors, and any problems of a structural (and therefore un-fun) nature seemed so lame as to temporarily disappear.

Al and I did a final walk-through, where I pointed out a few small things to be repaired before the papers were signed. And then there was nothing to do but await the closing.

The closing took place on a very hot day, and through a miracle of scheduling, I had also agreed to a job interview that morning at a magazine in Boston. I remember thinking, halfway through the interview, that I should slow down, that my interviewer didn't need to know every detail about the house and this big transition I was making and why I wanted to live in Providence—a whole state away—which was commutable but probably not an ideal location for their entry-level staff. I was loud; I was overheated in every sense of the word. I sweated through my trusty interview suit. I knew as I walked out the door that I would never be walking back in.

Then it was on to the main event—screw this job stuff, just let me buy this house! The closing happened at a small-town law office north of Providence. I changed out of my interview clothes in the car, took a couple of steadying breaths, and walked in. Al, the Unrealtor, and a host of lawyers and assistants, all seated around a beige conference table, turned to assess my entrance. Clearly having learned nothing from the morning's interview episode, I immediately began babbling, already well on my way to sweating through my fresh clothes despite the corporate-level air conditioning in the office. Quickly, an unthinkable number of very important, unintelligible papers were put in front of me. It would have taken days to read all of them, so I relied on the lawyers in the room to tell me what I was signing. I made clever jokes, congratulating myself on my ability to be funny even in a room with a bunch of lawyers. *Damn, you're charming*, I thought, then, *hold on—did I just catch that guy rolling his eyes at me?* I'm certain they discussed my unfortunate cocaine dependence after I left, but my high was all caffeine, stress hormones, and neurosis.

Driving off in my purple Honda, though, I couldn't have cared less about their forms and the lawyers and motivational wall art. I felt a fierce and thrilling delight at what I had just done, like I was flipping the bird at all of convention, because now I'd get to see this project through. Whatever the outcome, it was mine. After four months of dealing with Al and the Unrealtor, I was ready to see them back off and— for our purposes—cease to exist, so that James and I could get this experimental aircraft off the ground.

Three of Everything

We returned to the Boston apartment to pack up the rest of our stuff, including our two plump male cats, Kernel and Rocky, and then piled everything into a U-Haul. We slowly trundled the fifty or so miles south to Providence, jumping down from the truck to gaze at the largesse of this thing that was now mine: the two-toned aluminum siding a faded, sagey green on the ground floor, and white on the top two. Shielding my eyes from the sun, I wished out loud that whoever had owned this house in the fifties had never been visited by a siding salesman. James said, "I'm telling you, the wood's still under there. They usually just covered it up." Before I could object, he ripped a chunk of siding off the back corner of the house to prove his theory, and there it was: a tantalizing swatch of gray clapboard. It was pretty, not rotten; even the old (lead?) paint was intact.

I had no money to have the siding taken down and the old toxic paint removed—it was a fool's errand anyway, the costs likely to balloon into the tens of thousands, and for what tangible benefit? Meanwhile, my boyfriend had begun ripping pieces off the house we had yet to move a single box into.

James flung the aluminum off to the side, and we

started dragging our stuff over the threshold, a moment during which reality (*we live here now*) sent a momentary chill through the steamy August air. The house was in the barest state possible for our habitation. There was no gas or electric service; the walls, chalky plaster or bare drywall, were scratched; and we had twenty rooms, plus two sizeable stairwells, to prime and paint. It dawned on me, a little late, that there were three of everything—boilers, water heaters, toilets, sinks, stoves, fridges—and that any of those things could break now, in twenty minutes, in a week. Nothing looked finished; Al's guys had left jagged edges, chunks of plaster, and sawdust. The yard was filled with trash and weeds. It was hot and the air was dank; rats skittered outside; weird smells crept in.

We slept in the front room on the first floor for a while, too exhausted to move anything upstairs to the third floor, where we planned to live once we settled in. A reddish streetlight glow landed on me each night, and I'd lie in its pool feeling helpless—helpless in the house, with its unconquerable problems now becoming clear; helpless in my relationship, newly guided toward a distracting common goal that I worried would overcome us; helpless in this weird neighborhood that didn't feel at all like home. In the morning, that doomy perspective vaporized, but it left a haze of doubt.

My life's foundation was slipping out from under me, but I sought to steady it by decorating like nobody's business. After years of apartments painted entirely in Clinical White, or its skanky cousin Dirty

White, I wanted to paint every room a different highly saturated color. Luxuriating in paint chips, I could envision greatness. "You want to live in a goddamn roll of LifeSavers," James said, which sounded good to me.

Getting underway, we proclaimed our ignorance loudly and proudly by buying two giant barrels of oil-based primer, which adheres instantly to any surface it touches. Rather than wiping up easily, as with water-based primer, a mistake is simply smeared around ad nauseam. When applied via our signature slapdash painting technique, gobs of it splattered on the floor and were tracked around on our shoes or cats' paws, drying there into an indelible mess. We snipped at one another, our primer-laden rollers dripping on our shoes, already frustrated. He thought I was too slow; I thought he was too sloppy. I felt a shaky anger welling up whenever we tried to collaborate; why were we so inadequate at working together? Several couples I knew had bought and worked on their houses together; though they confessed that the process was hard, and things got heated from time to time, they didn't mention soul-crushing alienation and resentment. The admittedly too-perfect renovating couples who starred in their own half-hour look-how-well-that-worked-out shows on HGTV didn't allude to questioning the very structure of their own philosophies of self in the midst of a project. I felt it necessary to keep a lid on my feelings, knowing that airing them would cause a fight, which would then cause us to stop working, probably for days. We could not afford to clash on every decision. *I would rather be doing anything else*, I would think self-pityingly, and before long I added, *with anyone else*. I was taken aback by how quickly our enthusiasm threatened to tap out, and how close to the surface the tension felt.

From the street, PennHenge looks like a freakishly large tooth in a grinning mouth. It's crammed in between two smaller houses, and it's less than ten feet from the street, so it looms large, as if perpetually sneaking up on passersby. There's a length of electric-green chain-link fence at the property line, with a gate that straddles the concrete steps to the front door. The fence serves no purpose that I can ascertain, and can easily be skirted, but even as a largely mental barrier it seems to have kept the taggers from hitting the house; the buildings on either side are not so lucky.

The house's front entry is one of its best attributes—one of the surviving Victorian vestiges of its prettier past. French doors with dainty, white curtains open wide and provide a breezy gateway to a graceful winding stairwell. An ornate overhang, skillfully carved and painted white, crests the doors. It is lovely, but it's not functional. This is merely an ornamental doorway, not one used to actually enter and exit the building: the lock is sticky, the door is tricky, and because the key is long gone, we can only lock it from a bent antique latch on the inside. The doors' exteriors, too, are painted a thick green—someone in this house's past really loved all the sickliest options in the green universe—and the wood's pitted remnants imply decades of Providence rain, snow, and heat. Someone shot a BB through one of the panes of glass, and a diminutive hole remains.

We're going in. We've got to do it eventually.

The key turns in the lock; the back door squeaks open. In contrast to the rather grand front entry, this one is purely utilitarian. The floor, having just been stripped of its 1950s linoleum, is now rough, worn wood stained by years of humidity and salty winter boots. The heavy wood door to the first-floor apartment is just inside.

From the back door, one enters into the kitchen, which is dwarfed by boxy 1980s-era almond-colored appliances that wheeze and whirr and have already exceeded their life expectancy by several years. The floor is bowed in multiple directions, lending it a wavy quality that makes it difficult to decide where to stand. It is covered in fake terra cotta tile installed by Al's amateur contractors, so cheap and brittle that a few of the tiles have already cracked in half. Through a jaunty little arched doorway, there's a skinny pantry, with huge, old farmhouse-style cabinets, more cut-rate tile (this time used as countertop), and a dingy metal sink like the one in my second-grade art classroom that had tempera paint residue dumped in it year upon year.

Al's penny-pinching ways had pushed him to get creative, and now that we were in the house I saw how often he'd used materials for contraindicated purposes. Like a doctor who prescribes drugs for off-label usages a little too liberally, Al put tiles that were not meant to bear weight on the floors;

he put sheets of vinyl flooring on the walls as back-splashes (I caught that one early and made him take them down); he made "doors" for utility closets out of sheets of thin beaded plywood, leaving nails poking clear through to the other side. I got the feeling he had a stockpile of low-quality building materials that had to be used—somehow, any way they could be manhandled into place—before he would buy anything new. None of it would function for more than a year, but his objective had been to get the house sold and off his docket, and not to make a lasting home for anybody.

The first-floor bathroom is not exempt from this key tenet of Al's decorating bible. Kitchen flooring masquerades as bathroom tile; the light fixture belongs in a hallway, is not moisture-safe, and has the distinct look of being purchased in an economy twelve-pack. There's also a bleak peachy-colored one-piece shower/tub insert, like something you might find in a bummer motel. The toilet Al provided started leaking soon after move-in, so I had it replaced with a new one, a point of pride because—in the plumber's exact words—"you can flush a dozen golf balls down this thing."

The living room is in the middle of the apartment, with three bedrooms branching off from there. There's a tall bay window with four skinny panels; it looks out over the driveway, with the next house a confining ten feet away. The flooring might be nice, but it's tough to tell its true condition because it's been painted in many layers over the years.

The frontmost room in the apartment was intended to be a second living room—or "parlor," as they called it around here in the old days—used in quainter economic times for entertaining or family gatherings. But because the parlor is much larger than either of the two dinky original bedrooms, it makes more sense to use it as a bedroom. These two rooms are the grandest in the house, with their Victorian bay windows, pretty, white marble fireplaces, and crown moldings. The other two bedrooms on the first floor are fairly nondescript: boxy little ten-by-tens, each with a single window and a shallow closet.

Up the back stairs, which are so worn as to provide convenient hollows for one's feet to neatly fall into, and we're at the entrance to the second-floor apartment. The layout here is identical to that of the first floor, perhaps a bit less beat-up, but feeling equally empty and unfinished. The cumulative feel of these two apartments is that they are adequate for human habitation, but not at all shiny or sleek. The swankiest things on site are the old marble fireplaces, which no longer function as originally intended but would one day serve as pretty dope spots for my tenants' candles, animal skulls, and DVDs. There are no dishwashers, no garbage disposals, no exhaust fans in the kitchens or bathrooms. There is a comical dearth of electrical outlets; already we're running ten different power strips and extension cords.

James and I begin haphazardly arranging our things in the third-floor apartment, which consists of an adorable, if diminutive, five rooms: two small bedrooms, a living room at the small end of average, a large kitchen with a pantry, and a tiny bathroom. There's charming wainscoting in the kitchen; simple, timeworn shelving in the pantry; the bedroom ceiling is made up of angled eaves; and the apartment's got a general "cabin in the woods" feel, perched up above the urban fray. We liked the look of it at first sight.

As with many third-floor apartments in Providence and elsewhere, the kitchen is in the center, and the other rooms fan out from it. The flooring consists of commercial black-and-white vinyl tiles, the kind you'd see in a pizzeria or taco shop. There's a clunky white refrigerator and a 1950s Glenwood enameled metal stove that still works handily as a stove and an oven. It's a gas-on-gas stove, meaning it also contains a heater—the only heating "system" in the apartment. On one hand, it's charming and simple; on the other, we'll soon trust this antiquated technology to keep our toes from freezing.

Just off the kitchen, a small pantry with kitchen sink will be our storage spot for food, dry goods, dishes, tools, cookbooks. Thickly painted shelves are situated just above the sink and extend to the slanted ceiling, and another high shelf runs the length of the opposite wall. It's crowded and sort of falling apart, but I love this little glorified closet.

The bathroom, though, is distinctly unlovable. When friends come over to see the house, they go in to take a pee and come out shaking their heads. "I know," I say, "it's awful. Don't make fun of it." This room is a comedy of errors done up in porcelain and plastic. The black-and-white checkered restaurant floor is the same as that used in the kitchen, but is even less appropriate in a bathroom. The leaky plastic shower stall recalls summer camp nightmares; a mysterious door opens onto the back of the shower from the next room. The door to the bathroom doesn't quite line up with its frame, so it doesn't close all the way: a truly inhospitable feature to discover in one's new bathroom. Then again, the gap between the door and its frame is the only ventilation in the room, seeing as the single skylight window does not open. It becomes so hot in this room that taking a shit begets psychedelic visions. Sitting there in cathartic sweat, I'd think, *Am I being punished? Have I been a terrible human being?*

I'd been dreaming of the graceful surroundings of my new house, but for now I'd appreciably downgraded my living situation.

Sitting up at night, lonely, cracking a few beers, James drawing in the next room, I'd watch HGTV and reruns of *This Old House.* "It's all so *easy,* isn't it?" I'd mutter at the television. "You fuckers have no idea." This, of course, was untrue. Those fuckers had a TV budget, plus more skills and knowledge than I could ever glean from watching TV. They were professionals at this gig, and I was just playing at it, hanging on to the illusion that I was qualified to do so. I'd hungrily watch project after project line up perfectly on the first try, look beautiful, cause no stress, and cost more than my yearly salary. Nauseous, I'd click the TV off and curse the seemingly endless list of tasks ahead of me, along with my own ineptitude at getting them done.

It was during these first few weeks that I realized how little I knew about my new neighborhood. Federal Hill is a historically Italian American enclave, with a visitor-friendly main drag lined with restaurants, bars, very drunk people, very rude people, and shopping. But the instant you leave this little low-rent adult Disneyland, the neighborhood goes Wild West. I soon learned that social niceties were not valued in the Hill. Passersby parked facing the wrong way; blocked driveways; discarded food, trash, furniture, and mattresses in the street; laid on the horn; listened to thudding jams at ear-destroying volumes; rooted around in trash cans and cars. From the third floor, I had a great upper-deck seat for a few neighborhood-wide street brawls. People yelled for their friends instead of knocking on the door or ringing the bell, barking in the style of a kid looking for his mother's attention.

I come from a stoic New England family in which shouting is only to be employed in extreme emergencies. Even in a desperate crisis, many of my family members would only widen their eyes and murmur quietly. I had a laissez-faire attitude about the commotion; I didn't love it, but I wasn't overly upset about it. Then I began to consider who would want to pay good money to live here with me. Who would possibly volunteer to come along on this misguided fantasy ride? Could I be trusted with anyone's well-being? What if *everything* broke, right away? Until now, this whole "tenants" concept had been abstract. It was just how I planned to (eventually) pay the bills. Now, it was becoming clear that the strategy involved actual people. I was going to be the provider of basic shelter and conveniences for adults, kids, animals, potted ferns, and whatever else turned up. And I was going to have to find tenants before the first mortgage payment was due in a few short weeks.

I posted ads around town and on Craigslist for the two apartments, and fired up my loud mouth to start recruiting person-to-person. My friend Tamara, who'd occupied my room in the Boston apartment before I lived there, had also moved back to Providence and was very shortly to be married to her boyfriend, Jack. They wanted to move out of their place and start fresh in a new one. Considering there was no paint on the walls and there was still construction dust and debris everywhere, "fresh" was one way to say it. They saw past the apartment's very apparent shortcomings, and said they'd take the first floor for my asking price of $800 per month. They even offered to paint it themselves for a modest discount on the first month's rent. Feeling good, we settled on a move-in date in October. One down.

Since we'd left Boston, James had spoken with his friend Ben, a screenprinter and artist, and asked him to move into the house with his girlfriend Daria. Ben and Daria lived in a cramped space on the then-industrial Boston waterfront, which also housed Ben's printshop. Technically, they were not supposed to be living there at all—the space was designated as a studio only. Ben and Daria decided to escape the high-rent/low-opportunity vortex of Boston and move an hour south to much-cheaper Providence.

James and Ben could rent a bargain studio space and join forces to start up a new print shop. They plotted for days and weeks, and convinced Daria, a graphic designer, it would be a good move for her as well, though her lack of enthusiasm was palpable. With James and I promising prosperous times ahead, they agreed to leap with us, and to paint and do limited, small repairs on their place. Because they were doing us a favor of sorts, they rented the entire second floor at the absurd rate of $600 per month. This left me on the hook for about $600 a month on the total mortgage payment of about $2,000. Not quite "living for free," as James had assured, but at least the house would be full and the bills would be covered.

That autumn, as everyone moved in, routines emerged. The personalities meshed fairly well; my new tenants' complaints about each other were few, and mostly related to the sounds of late-night furniture arrangement. I was still commuting to my job as an editor just outside of Boston, so my life was composed of three tasks: getting to work, being at work, and coming home and not working on the house. All weekend, as I scraped off old paint, drilled holes in the wrong places, and swore at the cats—who inevitably made paw prints on everything with the ill-fated oil-based primer—I dreaded going to work on Monday. All week, as I dozed off at my desk, I dreaded having to return to rediscover the wonders of home repair.

I had become vaguely aware that I wasn't feeling

totally up to it all—my stomach hurt all the time and I was always in the bathroom. Wagon trains of pink rashes roved my skin, camping for a few days on one patch, a few days on another. I was drained of energy. My guts sputtered loudly all day long. I abandoned any semblance of a professional appearance at work by napping on the lawn directly faced by the company's office windows. My digestive issues were too gross to think about, so I decided they were a temporary stress response. I worried about the house, and money, and keeping it all together; my inner distress seemed a fitting result. I treated myself unforgivingly; because I had signed up for this lifestyle, I had to make it work. I would not let it fail. I just felt *tired*— more tired than I had ever been before.

At home, the work was slow-going, unskilled, and soul-sucking. Within a few months of moving in, I started to think I was too young to have so little fun. Suddenly I felt tied down by a bunch of adult bullshit. I'd somehow deluded myself into thinking it would all be fun. As anyone who has done this will tell you, the end result—having a comfortable, well-maintained, attractive place to live—is pretty great, if you ever get there. But nothing leading up to it is actually *fun,* especially if you are an amateur with little upper-body strength.

In my grandparents' time, of course, I'll bet I would've had a husband, two kids, *and* a house by age twenty-seven. And I wouldn't have had the luxury of complaining about having to be an adult. But I also probably wouldn't have had a full tilt, full-time job and a stressy commute. I also likely wouldn't have been the only one financially supporting the household.

Nonetheless, the work had to be done, and in response James and I took on the personae of two people stuck in an elevator: we were only working together in order to extricate ourselves from a problem. Trapped, we ground it out, sanding, painting, and fixing doorjambs. We thought our malaise as a couple was external and temporary; maybe once the bathroom was fixed or the dryer installed, we'd revert to loving one another.

When we tried to update even the simplest of items, though, we quickly learned that this house laughed in the face of modernization; its very beams and planks and every inch of its horsehair plaster rebelled against it. PennHenge knew it had the upper hand, that it was bigger and older than James and I were, and much more stubborn. Hardware store items marked "standard size" or "fits any ____" taunted from shelves; purchased with optimism, they quickly became nonstarters, tossed into a pile of other stuff that couldn't be bent or jammed into place. PennHenge and its neighbors were thrown together quickly and with more improvisation than would be considered acceptable by today's standards. This was economy housing, built speedily but with a kind of rigid integrity that made it heavy and immutable, even if its lines were imperfect.

On the first very cold day, sometime in mid-December, I was leaving the house when I heard the peculiar sound of rushing water coming from the basement. It didn't sound like the washing machine; it didn't sound like the shower lines. When I rounded the corner at the bottom of the stairs, I stopped in my tracks as I saw little waves lapping up against the bottom stair. Scanning the expanse of water between myself and the far wall, I found the source: the pipe leading to the washing machine had frozen, and an alarming amount of water was bursting forth. I sighed a single Zen "shiiiiiit" and ran back upstairs to cram on my rain boots.

James was at work. I didn't even consider calling him: this was a crisis, and there was no time to deliberate. Instead, I called Fred, my plumber friend, and asked him what I should do. I ran back down into the fray. He said slowly, without urgency, "Well, I wouldn't stand in the water if I were you; it could be electrified and you could electrocute yourself."

I shrugged. "Too late, dude. I'm already in it."

"Oh. Okay, then, no harm done I guess. So go over to the main water line, and shut it off."

"Any idea where that would be?"

"Uh, I don't know exactly, probably toward the front of the house."

I waded out and located the item in question. I had never noticed it before. It was a dirt pit with a single pipe sticking out of it, and a valve with a big red knob.

Fred said, "Turn that thing counter-clockwise as far as it will go. That'll shut off the water and you'll be able to call someone to fix the pipe." It dawned on me that I had to find a go-to plumber and I had no idea where to look in those pre-Facebook times, when the world was dark. The deluge slowed, the sloshing and dripping let up, and I stood there for a minute, shocked by the episode (but not by an electrical current). I experienced a momentary assortment of life-condemning thoughts, but then I discovered my single best landlady trait, the one natural attribute that qualifies me to do this job. Without thinking much about it, I became calm. My mind and my body relaxed into the task at hand, focused, facing it. The emergency portion of this thing had ended. Now all I had to do was clean up the water, call a plumber, and spend some money to fix the broken pipe. There was *nothing to freak out about.*

Shop-Vac in hand, suctioning dirty water, I amused myself by picturing the scene as an old maritime painting of a miniature boat manned by yellow-jacketed sailors, struggling against tiny whitecaps perched atop a dark, roiling sea. Having made it through the first misadventure, I thought, *Well, if that's all it is, I can handle this house thing.* Like the hardy sailors in my mind, I pictured myself struggling through the storm, persevering to face the next crisis. Sometimes that's what life is, and it's not as bleak as it sounds.

Renter-go-round

After a year at PennHenge, Tamara and Jack let
me know they were moving out. Jack came upstairs,
tapped on my door, and delivered the news with little fanfare: Tamara was pregnant. They needed to
be near her family. Moving on was a natural next
step. They'd had fun, but had to leave.

I closed the door and leaned on the wall. Nothing
in their departure implicated me as a bad landlady or all-around horrible individual. This was just
logistics. Somehow, though, I felt stunned, as if I'd
been dumped in the midst of what I thought was a
perfect relationship. I never expected them to stay
forever—renters are always moving, always seeking
a new city or situation. But now I saw the future,
and it promised rapid-fire move-ins and move-outs,
with brief moments of quiet in between. A year goes
by in a day. Everyone at PennHenge was straining
to leave adolescence, to feel sure of something for
once, and our lives were full of newness and babies
and breakdowns and breakups.

I had failed to visualize what it would be like to
live with tenants, and likewise, what it would be like
to watch them leave.

Even considering these first stirrings of upheaval,

I could feel good that we'd made it through a year. The lights were on and the bills were paid. But progress was slow, and the house was still in a state of raw need. For every fault we fixed, a new one was noted.

Having survived one winter with windows that could be open or closed with little change to the interior climate, James called a window salesman, a friend of his family. James had spent some time installing windows for his dad's home improvement company, so we had agreed to DIY this thing. Even so, we counted the number of windows in the house; the grand total was forty-three windows, and I feared the likely cost of replacing them, not to mention the time we'd need to invest to install them. Window Guy came and measured each one, the two of us following him around asking questions. Because James was once "part of the crew," we were granted the luxury of skipping Window Guy's full-bore sales pitch—the smoke and mirrors normally employed to plump the bill were nullified when you were speaking to someone from a contractor family. Still, the price tag to buy forty-three of the most basic model windows—white vinyl and white hardware with absolutely no ornamentation, including a discount and sans installation—was around $6,500.

James's brother, also a contractor, delivered the stacks of windows tidily wrapped in plastic. A salty bunch, he and his crew smoked and cracked jokes while they reviewed the process: remove the wood holding the old window in place and then remove the glass a pane at a time, fit the new window into the newly opened space, stuff the edges of the frame with as much pink insulation as it'll take, and put screws through the frame in the holes provided. After we got that part done forty-three times, we'd deal with replacing the inner frames, skinny wood pieces that served to cover the vinyl edge of the new window and the wisps of insulation stuffed into the crack. "Cool," I said, already doubting my own ability to handle a single window. We had a window install party, and a few friends donned their work gloves on a chilly Saturday for pizza, beer, and the thrill of manual labor.

That afternoon, the house a buzzy whirl of drill sounds, the grapevine turned up a couple. They showed up unannounced to look at the recently vacated first-floor apartment. We hadn't done shit other than to tell a few people that we had a place available, but the news had gone around.

Elvin and Caroline were impish and conspiratorial, a pair of fresh-faced cuties who were really into one another. Their jean jackets were stitched with doom metal patches; they looked mildly tough, but they smiled a lot. They came upstairs to talk to me—by then they'd already stopped in to check out the apartment, and decided they wanted it, no intervention needed on my part—and we spent ten minutes talking over the logistics of the move-in and the utilities and their two cats. Then they left, still adorable. James and I looked at each other, astonished: new tenants had simply fallen into our orbit—no sweating over Craigslist or tacking up flyers. We didn't even consider any further vetting. They wanted to live here, they weren't total ogres: good enough.

Out of forty-three windows, we got half done that day. The rest fell to James and me and our handiest tenant, who happily worked until his portion of the job was done. James and I were less prompt. For the next few months, whenever there was a spare hour or two, I'd tentatively bug him: "Do you, ah, do you think maybe we could do a window?" I felt I had to ask, although I was relieved when he'd say no. I was happy to stay inert, pushing the task away again and again. The remaining stack of windows taunted us; finally, it began to dwindle. The last two—well, the last two disappeared.

Having happily quit my Boston office job and draining commute, I'd begun working at a coffee shop and trying for freelance writing gigs. A tremendous pay cut was involved in adopting this newly relaxed, noncorporate lifestyle, but I figured there were always temp jobs should things become dire. I only knew that I wanted my time to be my own, I felt like garbage, and I couldn't stand another summer of yearning for the sun while ensconced in fluorescent cubicle lighting. I wanted to see if I could get a writing career going in any sense of the word, and I didn't mind living on the cheap while I attempted to scale the walls of the publishing world.

A timid, forlorn gastroenterologist had recently diagnosed me with irritable bowel syndrome (IBS). I found this diagnosis totally unsatisfying—basically he was telling me, "You're a nervous lady, and you poop a lot and we don't know why, so here's some pills. Eat more fiber." The pills were meant to slow my digestion, but they only dried out my mouth while my butt continued its spree unabated. I stopped taking them after a couple of weeks. Now that I was taking my stress level down a few pegs, and eating enough fiber to build a shed every week, I assumed I'd be feeling better soon.

One evening in December, I was working at the coffee shop, slapping stickers on to-go cups and listening to this one Pat Benatar record we played over and over (why "Hell Is for Children," I'll never understand). We were gabbing, relishing the slow period before we closed for the night. The phone rang, and my coworker answered it. She passed it over: "It's James."

"Hey."

"Hey. I have some bad news."

"Oh shit, okay, what is it?"

"Ugh. It's pretty bad."

"Oh my god, all right, what is it?"

"The house got broken into. I just got home, and the back door was wide open so I knew something happened. I can't tell what's gone yet. I called the cops."

I felt very hot and tingly, suddenly hyperaware and ready to tip into a rage.

"Fuck. No! I'll be home in five minutes."

"Okay. Just so you know, it looks pretty crazy. The apartment doors are kicked off the hinges."

I pulled shakily into the driveway and entered what had become an unfamiliar place. All three apartments had been overturned, our stuff rifled through, drawers dumped and mattresses upended. James was assembling a quickly growing list of the things taken: tools, a table saw, my broken laptop, a TV, an elderly digital camera, guitars. The last two replacement windows were also gone—an especially irritating loss considering they were measured to fit the windows in my apartment and wouldn't work well anywhere else. My gym bag containing a sweaty sports bra and the ugliest capri-flare kelly-green sweatpants ever created. As James had warned me, the doors to all three apartments had been kicked in; the ones that had come clear off the hinges had been picked up by the intruders and placed against the wall. Looking for any potential clues of the burglars' humanity, I chose to believe that this door-leaning meant they still had a shred of caring, that this had been a crime of desperation and not one undertaken with unnecessary cruelty.

The dismantling of the doors shook me more than the loss of our stuff—none of it was of much value except for the guitars, which were not expensive but carried emotional weight. James and I made a doleful trip to Home Depot to buy every type of bolt, bar, and latch we could put our hands on, but it haunted me that anyone of reasonable strength could get in with a pair of steel-toed boots and a little motivation. Another chain on the door wasn't going to hold anyone off. We could only hope to subsist on our sparseness; there was nothing much left to take on a repeat visit.

The police were of little help; a cop came, hours after the fact, and yawned his way through a laundry list of questions. I know these guys deal with burglaries every day, and it becomes a ho-hum endeavor to investigate them, but this officer seemed to believe that my simply living in this neighborhood meant I should expect to be violated early and often. Somewhere around "Well, you know, you moved to this street, it's rough out here," I checked out, plunking myself on the couch, hand to forehead, unable to expend the suddenly unthinkable level of effort it would take to refute him.

This became a common refrain of life at Penn-Henge for me, a single white woman with a fairly wispy appearance. The (usually white) men who come to the house in some service capacity—plumbers, cable guys, cops, electricians, contractors—have often been perfectly comfortable commenting to me on the unsuitability of the neighborhood for "someone like" me. Most of the time this disapproval takes the form of a gruff sadness: "It's too bad what's happened to this place—the drugs, the crime. It used to be so nice." Less commonly, but still alarmingly often, it is a panicky racist rambling, a fear-steeped monologue that surfaces as soon as the man realizes I'm friendly, a talker, possibly a willing sieve for his opinions. Before I can get my bearings, the guy is going on about "the blacks, the Muslims . . ." and I'm backing toward the door. I only wanted the toilet fixed, bro.

A Cambodian American man I know, a guy of about fifty, born and raised in Providence, asked me where I live. First, he congratulated me on owning a place in a trending neighborhood in town, a place where property values are climbing after having topped out in the tonier, dog shit-free areas of town.

We talked about that for quite some time. Then, almost as an afterthought, he told me that when he was a teenager, I suppose in the seventies, he and a bunch of Cambodian friends tried to go to some Italian festival on the Hill, and were violently chased out of the neighborhood. He softly chuckled as he recalled the details.

I mentioned the story and his calm retelling of it to an acquaintance, who said, "Oh yeah, people of color were not allowed into Federal Hill until recently. It was just *known*." A chilling choice of words—"not allowed." Only recently did I begin to understand what this wistful "old neighborhood" parlance stands for: the time before Providence's densest neighborhoods were available to people of color. The time before white families left; before the neighborhood became what it is today: a multicultural zone comprised of people of all racial, ethnic, and economic backgrounds. Is that what these men were harkening back to? Is there coding in the tsk-ing and the "so sads"? Is their protective pity talk born out of something nastier than just pathetic nostalgia?

This shit is just swirling all around us, every day, in this city, state, and country.

And yet, I still need to get the toilet fixed. How diplomatic can I be and still let such a man know that I do not agree with him, that I've lived in the neighborhood for a decade, that it suits me quite well, that I respect my neighbors and do not wish for a reversion to the old days of quiet tyranny and wall-to-wall white in Federal Hill? That if there's a reason to get out, it's the house itself, and not the people with whom I share the street?

Elvin and Caroline hadn't been in the house long when the break-in happened; I was mortified that this was their intro to living at PennHenge. They were grossed out by the intrusion, and they were annoyed that they'd lost things. I was afraid they'd move out, but they seemed to take it in stride. They continued to settle in, putting up leopard print curtains and arranging their old furniture and one million VHS tapes, DVDs, CDs, and records. They tacked up rock show and movie posters. The cats continued to familiarize themselves with the apartment; the humans sank into the couch and began the continuous movie marathon that defined their home life. If they were home, there was a movie on— the weirder the better. They were sweet people who liked dark shit. And not just in their choice of filmed or recorded entertainment; they both had a potent somber side that ruled them as much as their funny irreverence. These two seemed *united* by dark shit, as if their gloom was their central connection. Not to say they weren't also a good time. We had boozy all-night backyard fires that often ended in some innocent object—a chair, usually—getting tossed into the blaze, or in Caroline baying at the fire on hands and knees, the strands of her long hair whipping just out of the flames' reach.

On the plus side, the break-in provided a springboard for me to meet my neighbors on one side, an elderly Italian couple named Angelo and Fiorella. They'd emigrated from Italy to the United States in the sixties, and had lived on Penn Street ever since. I had stealthily admired Angelo's stunning head of thick, lustrous white hair from our third-floor window, which overlooked the concrete and dirt lot where they were often at work on one project or another. I knew they'd been observing us too, this band of strange folks who'd been making noise in (but also slowly beautifying) the house next door. Since they spoke rapid-fire Italian together, and seemingly no English, I figured we'd not get to be friends. But one afternoon I went outside, and through a broken slat in the fence, Angelo introduced himself and his wife. I had trouble understanding his accent; he either said he'd heard the break-in in progress, or he'd heard about it from someone. Either way, he was none too happy about it or "these bad people" who'd steal anything they could put their hands on. He was happy to see we were in the house, though, as it had been empty for a long time, the old windows left wide open and the rain coming right in. (I knew then why some of the windowsills were cracked and falling apart.)

Angelo's account of PennHenge's utter neglect in recent years made me morbidly curious as to what other surprises awaited us. I felt, viscerally, all of those bad years then; when I entered the house I smelled abandonment, and once you've noticed that scent, it's not easy to forget. In every puckered spot on the plaster and every cracked floorboard, I saw a symptom of the inattention that had long resided here, and I wanted to fix it all, to restore the house to a gleaming past I had fabricated for it.

Around the same time as Elvin and Caroline's arrival, Ben and Daria, the Bostonian artist/graphic designer couple, gave me their notice. They were breaking up and moving—separately—to the West Coast, one to southern California and one to the Pacific Northwest. James and Ben weren't meshing all that well in their new print shop, and they too were ready to cut ties. "Guess the house killed *that!*" James and I joked as they prepared to move out. The tenant carousel continued to turn a bit too quickly for me, but I was new to the game then, and beginner's luck was with me.

That summer, among other jobs, I worked selling vegetables at a farmer's market once a week in downtown Providence. Riding my bike home with twenty dollars and a tote bag full of leafy splendor, carrot greens brushing my neck, sniffing the cooling evening air, pinned me like a dagger to Providence. I was feeling out my lucky freedom, learning how to move within it.

One sunny afternoon at the market, a guy sauntered up between the bunches of radishes and started chatting with my coworker, saying he was looking for a place in town. Something about the way Nick approached and the way he spoke, in combination with his dark hair and obscure band T-shirt and dirty jeans and the general air of summery farmer's market fleshiness, made him electrically attractive to me. This was a novel delight considering my tattered relationship with James, which was enfeebled but soldiering on. Nick and I had a smiling, easy conversation, interrupted at intervals by customers holding out bunches of kale. It was thrilling. It had been a long time since I had felt such a charge.

Being a champion hider of love interest, though, I kept this sudden flush to myself and switched to business mode, asking him what he was looking for (cough) and how soon he could move (ahem).

Within a few weeks, Nick carted in his books and guitars and jars of herbs and more pairs of dirty jeans. He fashioned his apartment in true anarcho-hippie style: simple furniture, neat unfinished wood shelves full of very smart books, a desk at which he drew and wrote letters to far-flung anarchist friends, plants everywhere. A sort of sun-warmed, mellow glow fell upon the place.

Nick and I became friends instantly. That was another surprise. There was little need for us to figure one another out, to gauge pros and cons, because we just got along, no adjustments required. Not one to seek complications, I kept the attraction on the back burner of a stovetop in another dimension. I wasn't in love with him; I only needed to avoid accidently falling onto his penis. There had been no clues toward a mutual attraction, so it seemed we could keep it simple.

Nick worked at a coffee shop and a record store, always under the table. He wanted to be untraceable: no authority would know he existed. He didn't vote, had no credit cards and no bank account, and stayed out of the burgeoning trappings of social media. He sat tight and stayed focused on what was in front of him. He had a romantic notion of the road and a deadly serious respect for freedom and anonymity. But he was also funny, an expert in good-natured razzing grounded in truth. He liked precision; he liked his world just so, an old man in training.

With Nick, James, and another friend or two, I'd frequent the witchy little herbal apothecaries that used to exist in Providence. We'd go in search of herbal medicinals: kava, mallow, St. John's wort. We'd gaze at the crystals, read the runes, and sniff the incense. Nick bought herbs for tea and tincture making, brought them home to end up in brown dropper bottles for quick flicks under the tongue.

There was a dignified simplicity to having Nick in the house. He quickly became the best tenant yet: considerate, loyal, caring, a tinkerer who was happy to make repairs. He took responsibility without acting like he owned the place. We often left the house in Nick's charge when we went away; we knew we could trust in his conscientiousness. I also may have deeply sniffed his laundry on occasion as I removed it from the dryer to make room for my own. And every once in a while I'd imagine a situation in which he and I might find ourselves locked in a closet, or the basement, or some other confined space.

He could be the model tenant in every way, and still I would picture him as something else entirely.

The Wolf of Penn Street

As the sweet summer unfolds and I inch the windows open, guzzling the newly languid, heavy air of warm weather, the first few startling booms seem like an anomaly. But all through June, the sounds of sputtering, sizzling, and blasting ramp up, getting closer together and then overlapping, until the night of the Fourth of July, when James and I count the seconds of quiet between the fireworks and rarely get past three. The spent bits pelt the roof and the sidewalk, ding off the siding, and land in the driveway. There is a gleeful fury to this takeover of the streets. I complain; I cannot think. To me it sounds less like celebrating and more like simulating the sounds of a warzone. I thank luck and accidents of time that it's only the *sound* of warfare that I'm forced to tolerate; then, as night passes into morning and the flashes and blasts slow down, I drift into a sweaty besieged sleep worried that a flaming projectile is going to come through the open window. I dream that the house is quickly filling with large insects that I must brush off the walls and sweep in wriggling piles off my bed.

Independence Day. July Fourth. It's been almost two years since James and I moved into the house.

It's become familiar, this routine of paying the mortgage and sweeping the floor and coming home from the coffee shop to make soy meatballs and pasta. Finding James at his desk, facing the wall, drawing and scratching his head. Guessing that he watches porn after I go to bed. Not talking about much. Not knowing how our relationship will end, but knowing that it should. Holding on because I don't want to be alone; not realizing that I am already alone. The booming summertime onslaught sucks any negative space out of the house; along with the trapped third-floor heat, it makes the air too dense for thinking. I subsist on ice chewed from a giant plastic cup, drape myself over the couch, make frustrated sounds.

The fireworks begin again in the early afternoon of July 5. I'm unable to function. Using my last measure of energy, I gather myself up and decide to meet the fray head-on. A bike ride. I get on my squeaky red eighties Fuji and whisk my way around the neighborhood. *There is always this*, I tell myself. Breeze and space and people moving around. Street trees swaying. The houses all opened up, people in their driveways or on their front stoops. The fireworks are still startling, but my own movement makes the sound feel less confining. A little of the tension melts off. I grip the handlebars less tightly, start to smile at the kids. I think about how we all ended up here.

Federal Hill, this ragged cluster of streets just west of downtown Providence, once grew too fast, then shrank too fast, and then grew back rather crookedly. Hosting 125 years or so of too-close human habitation, without adequate oversight or upkeep, can do that. The place has a shocked look, like the punches of recent history came too quickly to react.

Having originally been settled by English and then Irish immigrants, Federal Hill's population trickled upward in the late 1800s, when Italian immigrants began to arrive. By 1950, having hosted three surges of immigration, Federal Hill was suddenly home to over fifty thousand Italian Americans, who were now stacked and tucked into every available space. Families and landlords built and subdivided ever more houses, closer together, to contain them. On the first level of many triple-deckers, brick storefronts showcased family-run businesses—produce merchants, butcher shops. That year, at the peak of the immigrant boom, 20 percent of the city's population was shoehorned into this little neighborhood of three hundred acres, having quickly urbanized the land to the extreme. The Hill was an insular hamlet where one could get just about anything one needed to run a household, where the fruit and vegetable market was the beating heart of the community, and where irrefutable closeness and hostility connected the families, the New World version of an Elena Ferrante novel.

The growth and the decline of the neighborhood were equally swift. The congestion and heavy industry were too much, and people followed the general national trend, moving out to the suburbs in droves. The neighborhood lost a third of its population by 1960. The local mill economy was slowing, and factories were diminishing their workforces or moving out of town. Young Italian Americans were going off to college and moving into professional careers, not working in factories as their parents had. Several mild suburban towns saw entirely new neighborhoods of tidy, single-family ranch houses spring up, which the city-weary happily christened with Sunday gravy and fat sweet sausages frying in cast iron. These neighborhoods seem fairly hellish and samey and depressing to me now, but back then— such a luxury! No more urban grime and noise. It must have been a huge mark of success to have one of these homes, plenty to eat and a new car in the driveway.

People also sought suburban quiet because of the torment of the Mafia. A core group of connected men ran the neighborhood and oversaw mob activity in New England and beyond from a little storefront on Atwells Avenue, the Main Street of Federal Hill. The whiff of organized crime was subtle but constant, and unmistakable; just going out to get soap for the wash, for example, a lady could easily stumble upon something she wasn't meant to see. Playing nice with this crew was undoubtedly a big part of getting by in the Hill—and an enormous source of stress for those who even hinted at pissing them off. Not that they couldn't find you out in the suburbs, had you run afoul of the rules, but at least you'd be less likely to get caught in the crossfire. You wouldn't have to be at ground zero, absorbing the mayhem every day.

Though the mob's ironclad hold over the neighborhood has weakened substantially in the last thirty years, with deaths and indictments at the top of the chain, the mythology of this unsavory past has imprinted itself on the local psyche, morphing into a chuckling nostalgia and a collective overlooking of the heinous historical details. The mob is now relegated to a new status as feeble sideshow tourist attraction—a local sandwich shop called Wise Guys Deli does its logo up à la *The Godfather*; its motto is "Leave the gun. Take the sandwich." Hence, Atwells Avenue today: a strollable menagerie of Italian American food, "quirky locals" with heavy accents, and bars—some sleek and expensive, others carrying distinct possibilities for witnessing a stabbing. You can take your grandma here for her birthday lunch, or you can come here with your buddies looking to get loaded and grab ass. You can get a nice veal parmigiana, or you can get weed, coke, heroin. Assaults, stabbings, and shootings come in waves, although the city has revoked nightclub licenses to curb the violence; zoning changes in the past couple of years have curtailed the expansion of the bar scene as the city tries to funnel Federal Hill business back to more innocent entertainment: burgers, hookahs, and good ole Italian food.

In the 1980s and 1990s, the Hill hollowed out. White people in the Hill were resigned to coexisting with the mob, but once people of color started to move in, they couldn't get out fast enough. The remaining people with money left, fleeing to the beckoning suburbs. The Hill was becoming a place of transience and absentee landlordism where cheap apartments turned over once a year or more. Once-bustling houses, now aging poorly, went up in flames or were torn down by the city. Others went into disrepair and were abandoned. Thirty years later, we're still climbing out of that same pit. The neighborhood reinvents itself—but timidly, and on a tight budget.

The way many Rhode Islanders tell it, the post-Mafia years saw the Hill become a "bad neighborhood," full of "drugs and crime," though really, who could argue that a place terrorized for decades by everyday brutality hadn't been a bad scene all along? One type of lawlessness paves the way for its successor. But local lore says that in the old days, the neighborhood policed itself; if you stayed clean you had nothing to worry about. You simply let these guys carry out their nasty business all around you, pretending not to see a thing. These days, long-dead mob bosses are eulogized as having hearts of gold, their brutality only a minor personality trait among their good deeds benefiting average families around town.

When I moved into my house, a friend said, "Hey! You moved to Penn Street? I saw my first dead body on Penn Street in the nineties!" He wasn't joking. My mom monitors the news, helpfully letting me know each time someone on the street commits a crime or is released from prison: "Did you know you have a murderer on Penn Street?"

PennHenge, built just as the Italian population was really starting to swell, has stood through it all. This beleaguered house is still here, home to a number of people the original occupants of the house would likely find strange and scandalous. It existed through the heyday, the boom, the rapid decline, the years of Mafia rule, the neglect-ridden latter twentieth century, the recent recession, and now—improbably—here it is, ever so shyly dipping into a new century of who knows what. These days, there are only around eight thousand souls living on the Hill—less than one-fifth of the neighborhood's former girth—but it's a well-mingled mix of families, students, and just plain people from a healthy array of ethnic, racial, and economic backgrounds. This level of diversity seems to be accidental—it's probably caused by a combination of factors: proximity to downtown and the colleges, a high ratio of multifamily to single-family houses, and a fairly stable number of owner-occupants who doggedly hold on to their houses. And even if I stumbled onto the neighborhood also by accident, that's a quality that keeps me here.

Just about every surface in Federal Hill is coated in either concrete or vinyl siding. Vacant dirt lots and neglected patches of scruffy grass make up the difference. Knowing little first-hand about the good old days of the neighborhood, I'm free from wishing for them. Instead, I enjoy our current location on the continuum of history: we may be on the far side of glory, but there's something profound about living with the phantasms of the past, the empty faces of boarded-up houses calling us to make something of them once more. I used to see just the trash and the graffiti and the dog shit, and think this place might be a lost cause. But the more I interact with it, the more the neighborhood shows me that it may not be clean or beautiful, but it is a valid home. It is a place of fortitude with an undercurrent of unlikely kindness, a connectedness, where you can look people in the eye and say hello and they put everything aside to engage with you somehow.

Moving constantly—always seeking out a new home, a new city, a new job or lover to pull up roots for—is a state of being that alludes to upward mobility. It's akin to our culture's obsession with busyness and the pervasive inkling that we are only worthwhile when we are producing something. Moving a lot, whether between neighborhoods or cities or regions, signals that you are a seeker. You are not content to take what's placed in front of you, because you are a mover. Staying in one place—staying at rest—is to our modern minds sad and unambitious; it's a thing you do when you have nothing else to do.

But being a stayer means making a commitment to sit your ass down and wrestle with the realities of your chosen location; it means you face all of that and get discouraged and maybe bored, but you stay anyway—sometimes by choice, sometimes not—and in time you start to see through to the heart of it.

The opportunity to craft solid, long-term friendships—to get deep with one's community—is the single biggest benefit of being a stayer. I've heard new Providence residents remark with surprise that they see the same people everywhere, over and over, and that such a social setting takes getting used to. "You know, small town problems," they say, as if it's a liability. But I love it. I know that I can post up at a coffee shop and see a dozen friends. I step out of the house every day knowing that I'll run into someone

I really want to see, and possibly someone I don't. But the best part is, it's a time to interact without organized socializing. I don't need to present myself.

Providence is a small city, delineated into diminutive neighborhoods, and delineated further by our own visions of it; most of us who live here see "the neighborhood" as the street we live on, and everything else within about a three-block radius. Basically, if I can't see it from the third floor of my house, it's not in my neighborhood. Adjacent streets can be polar opposites; within a two-block radius from my own home are big, opulent single-family historic manors with landscaped grounds, as well as hulking, vinyl-covered apartment dwellings dotted with graffiti, porches sagging, shingles coming loose, going unrepaired year after year.

With its buildings generously twenty feet apart, Federal Hill forces disparate lives closer together. This is its beauty: my immediate neighbors are an elderly Italian couple with a fat little butter-colored terrier, a sweet, tight-knit Guatemalan family, a young Asian couple with a Shiba Inu, a Cape Verdean landlord whose multiple houses are always under construction, and some friendly, partying white kids a few years post-college age. Considering we're packed like freeze-dried coffee, we get along well. We don't bicker like they do out in the suburbs; nobody, in fact, has time for that. We all live our lives within our meager squares, and we let others do the same. Sometimes we even talk to one another through our jagged chain-link fences.

That said, our proximity to one another means we

don't attempt to hide the gross stuff. In the driveway of my own house, I've tripped over balled-up poop-heavy diapers, half-eaten food, dead birds, condoms, various pieces of clothing and underwear. I've found guys rooting around in my garage and peeing in my driveway at 2:00 a.m. Once, the morning after a late-night manhunt, during which the cops insisted on conducting a sweep of my basement and the first-floor apartment, I realized that the fugitive had been hiding out in my garden when I spotted squished tomato plants, his big footprints having mashed the soft soil.

One particular incident showed me the depth of my neighbors' goodwill. Where it runs alongside the house, the driveway at PennHenge is wide enough for one vehicle to pass through. A friend needed to park a medium-sized U-Haul truck in the driveway overnight. As he drove in, I noted a little too late and with some degree of horror that the U-Haul was only a couple of inches on one side from the house, and had the same short distance from the fence on the other side. This was fine for pulling in, where the view was clear and no rearview mirrors were needed, but it portended a precarious way back out. The next morning at 0700 hours, he jumped in and started inching the too-big truck back toward the thinnest section of driveway. Every time the truck would creep near to the house, I would yelp like an injured animal. There was no way we could do this without hitting something. Going back and forth with miniscule changes in tire direction did little to improve the odds. Finally, I coached him to just keep going, knowing full well he would run over a metal fence post, which responded by popping out of the ground at a high velocity, hitting the neighboring house with a resounding *ping!* and then a metallic clatter as it crashed to the concrete. The sleepy-eyed teenager whose bedroom we'd unintentionally missiled opened his window, stuck his head out, and—completely unperturbed, like this was how he woke up every day—said, "Yo, what was that?"

We explained. We apologized. We all laughed about it. My friend left a contrite note and a grocery store gift card in the family's mailbox, the latter of which they graciously declined when the dad of the house wrote his own kind note back to us. Eventually, we had a metalworking friend come over and weld the post back onto the base. It was like the whole incident had never happened, except that I loved my neighbors even more for being so understanding about these two jokers shooting a large metal projectile at their house at 7:00 a.m. Cheers to neighbors who know how to Let. Stuff. Go.

The neighbors may have been lovely, but PennHenge was throwing insults. It had been raining for two weeks. I returned home looking forward to cranking up my heating pad and taking a leaden nap on our huge old multicolored Grandma couch. Instead I found a three-foot hole in the ceiling and a pile of faintly musty, incredibly heavy plaster. There's a particular loneliness that comes with returning home to find that your living room ceiling is lying on the floor in dampened chunks. As I vacuumed the horsehair and tiny crumbles that had come loose, I could at least be thankful that we weren't home when it fell, and that one of the cats hadn't chosen that spot for a nap. But this was not good. There was in this experience both an urgency and a futility. I now had irrefutable evidence of the roof's dire status, which had begun to invade our personal space. I also felt a total lack of interest in this project, in doing all the little things it would take to make it happen. I couldn't afford it, I didn't know who to call, and what was the difference, the house was a heap I had overpaid for anyway. Who was I kidding with this homeownership thing? I was so tired. I turned off the vacuum cleaner and took the nap anyway.

When I woke up, the hole was still there. And now it was dripping.

Since the cost of replacing the windows had cleaned me out, I was back at zero dollars and looking to drum up some cash. I didn't know yet how much a roof would cost, but I knew James's brother, Shane, would be doing ours, and he would bust it out as cheaply as he could, but he had to be paid up front, no credit. I also knew that under normal conditions putting on a new roof was about the most expensive routine thing you could do to a house. But I wasn't going to do this on coffee shop money: I had a sweet new freelance writing job, at which I was flying blindly but enthusiastically. I was writing copy for a local web design company run by the nicest and fairest people imaginable. The pay was great, the hours were whenever, the attitude was wry. They designed the site interface, and then gave me the pages on which I would deign to create the most showstopping copy ever written about an alumni association. Staring at these blank-as-fuck pages for hours on end, sometimes something good flashed into my brain. Other times, it was an exercise in mediocrity. It wasn't exactly researching climate change in Brazil for the *Atlantic*. But I was writing for a living, in an unscheduled fashion, with good people, being prodded on by the angry hole in my living room ceiling that now dripped rust-colored water into a bucket whenever it rained.

Months later, the money was stockpiled and schedules aligned. The price for a new roof (and two new skylights that cranked open, to replace Al's sealed-shut miser model) would be $7,500. I went downtown to get a building permit, where they thought I was lying about the cost of the job in order to lower the price of the permit—"It should be twice that, at least," snorted the dude in charge. "Well, it's good to have a roofer in the family," I shot back. Considering the hijinks these bureaucrats must see every day in this little corrupt jewel of a city, my roof—even if I had lied about the cost—was a piddling matter, so they took my money and gave me the permit. I proudly went home and tacked it up in a front window as requested, feeling very boss.

A couple of days later, the crew showed up in white vans, ready to rock. I looked out to spy them standing on the sidewalk dragging on prework cigarettes and draining white Styrofoam cups of Dunkin' Donuts coffee. There were five or six roofers, a variety of ladders and tools, and piles of bundled shingles. Watching them unload, the enormity of this vertiginous job hit me: a bunch of guys are going to carry sixty-pound bundles of shingles up to my very, very high, sloped roof, from where they will literally be able to spit down onto the roofs of the houses on either side? I stuffed down my nausea and tried to be like them: 100 percent unfazed. Goofing and conducting intriguing manversations, they got right to work, tearing off the old, damaged roof in a couple of hours and putting down a protective layer of waterproofing. By the end of the first day, they had a portion of the new roof on. By early afternoon on the third day, the job was done. They swept up the scraps and left, while I marveled at the looks of what I'd just bought: snug, solid, just about impermeable to the elements.

I wondered what Shane had done to keep the costs so low. Did he pay his crew less than the usual rate? Did he use leftover shingles? Did he forego his own paycheck for the job, for his brother's old lady's sake? Or were the other roofers marking up their services just that much? He didn't talk about money; he didn't want to negotiate. He gave us a straight-up, rock-bottom price and I disbursed it gladly, paying my respects to the brusque and opaque ways of the roofer's code of honor.

I could now put the bucket away, though the living room ceiling hole persisted. I would no longer be tortured by the steady *plunk, plunk, plunk* of my house slowly drowning itself. But the experience had started up a simmering anxiety that made me strain my eyes and ears to search for new ruin.

I heard the *plunk, plunk, plunk* long after it had ceased, though there was no bucket to plunk into, and no drip to do the plunking. As I watched TV or read a book on the couch, my eyes would drift magnetically up to the hole. I'd look at it with detached scorn, like, *Someone really should get it together and fix that.* I just couldn't imagine that that someone was me. Hadn't I already done enough? What more did this house want from me?

Digging Down

The shock of moving into a house in bare need of some very basic things had absorbed my available brain matter for a couple of years, but the next spring—as the weather went from icy to steamy in the space of a week, as is the norm in these parts—I remembered with dread and excitement that I was also responsible for resurrecting a scrubby, trash-plastered dirt lot that I hoped someone might someday call a backyard.

I didn't know what I had or where to begin. The little square of land under my care was scarred and empty, as if torched by a fireball: scraggly, knee-high weeds reaching forth from scratched-up dust; a broken chain-link fence bisecting the small space—perhaps a former dog pen; faded bits of trash snagged in every corner; and dozens of little cellophane crack bags tumbling in the wind.

But the lower the nadir, I told myself, the more dazzling the opportunity for transformation. I was going to reform this delinquent land! I was going to bring it back from ruination!

I went to a used bookstore and bought books on organic gardening. I read blogs. I observed people around me who were building pretty and productive urban gardens—which were still a bit of a novelty in this time just before the locavore/farm-to-table/neo-hippie movement took full hold. Plus, crucially, my ace in the hole: I had friends who were starting up careers in farming and landscaping, who could be persuaded to help save a smidge of urban land from a dire state of affairs.

An old friend and her husband had just started a landscape design business. As a belated house-warming gift, they offered to draft a plan to revive my apocalyptic little yard. I rattled off my priorities: plants native to the area; tall, fancy grasses; space for vegetable beds and leeway around the fire pit James was planning to build; skinny pines that would screen out some of the nastiness of the parking lot behind the chain-link fence. The entire yard is something like twenty feet wide by fifty feet long, so we had to keep it tight and tidy. They prepared a master plan for the "Warner Residence" that detailed what they would do with the space, given my desired features and a total disregard for financial constraints. It was beautiful, visionary, and—even they admitted—maybe a little much. But they were giving me a provisional plan, they said, and I could leave out any parts that didn't suit me.

James and I decided to follow the basic shape of the plan, and to at least put the plants they recommended in the places they recommended. The rest—fancy stone inlays, timber bed edging, a pea-stone-filled patio surrounded by dense plants and arborvitae trees—we'd see about later on and probably never. I spent a dreamy afternoon at the nursery, getting grandiose in my mind and optimistically picturing myself in a chaise lounge under a thick canopy of glossy leaves, the scent of geraniums infusing the Tom Collins in my hand. *There are a few steps between here and there,* I thought. *First, you have to buy the plants, woman.* I selected them haltingly, enjoying their names (heavy metal switch grass, gayfeather, fothergilla, meadow rue) and blankly taking a stab at a substitute species when I couldn't find the exact one on the list.

James dug the fire pit and lined it with old cobblestones we got from the public works department of a neighboring town for a dollar each. I borrowed a tiller for the topsoil, and we turned the whole yard into a mud pit so that new grass seed could be put down. Contrary to our collaborations on indoor projects, James and I found cooperation easier when we worked outside. There were fewer rules in the garden, and we felt less pressure to be exact. We could be creative without worrying that we were compromising the integrity of some important structure. And we could be under the sun, gloves on, happily ankle-deep in the muck we were learning to tend.

The whole PennHenge crew helped us plunk the plants into the ground. The ten arborvitae trees, with their big burlap-wrapped root balls, were dunked into the dirt as well, watered liberally, and left to take hold. The whole setup looked a bit half-baked that year; amateur landscaping needs substantial settling time.

We battened down for the winter and hoped that everything would survive.

By April, all but one of the arborvitaes had died horrible, crispy deaths.

Point taken. No trees. Got it.

All of the smaller perennials made it, though, and as I went out to the yard to do the landscaper's walk of shame—digging up the root balls of the very dead trees that had been so alive just a few short months before—I doubled down on my dream of making this bedraggled dirt pit beautiful and productive. To my glee, a couple of bona fide farmers—my affable friend and erstwhile coworker Dean and his bighearted girlfriend Cal—had just moved in with my anarchist crush, Nick. Dean and Nick went way back. Dean had introduced me to Nick that day at the farmer's market, and now he and Cal were following him to PennHenge. It was perfect. I was so proud of the assemblage of quality people living in my home.

Dean and I had gotten to be buddies while working at the farmer's market, where we spent happy hours dissing the crabby customers while chomping reject cucumbers. Dean, a wiry, sweet guy with an unhurried air and a fondness for old Appalachian folk music, and Cal, a badass beauty from Baltimore with an effervescent laugh and a goofball sense of humor, arrived in a good-natured cloud of doggy dust (they had three between them), sweet music (they sang and played together), and crates of kale. They were starting up fledgling farming careers, and they'd drive off in a white truck with Dean's pitbull mix every day to the rented land they farmed. I was surprised that they wanted to live in the city—especially in my crowded and chaotic neighborhood—and commute to this beautiful expanse of land, but they had a lot of friends nearby and the price was right. Although they were moving in the direction of a rural lifestyle in the long run, they were entrenched for now in an urban one, and they liked the half-on-the-farm, half-off life.

Dean did not sweat the demise of the arborvitaes; he was more about efficiency than fashion. In their place, he mapped out a veggie garden. He planned and built two long and narrow raised beds, each twelve feet by three feet or so; we added clean soil from a pristine rural place to get around the problem of our certainly polluted, potentially lead-tainted industrial dirt.

We joked about dead bodies; secretly I was slightly anxious that we might encounter one. In the heart of a former mob-controlled neighborhood, digging down is a dicey prospect.

Dean and Cal started me off with some basic crops—easy stuff like greens, onions, cucumbers, and herbs. They ran through the rhythms of gardening—the cycles of planting, fertilizing, watering, harvesting, composting—and it blew my mind. We started a hack compost pile, and I bought some tools and books to keep around. I bought a couple of strawberry plants and hoped they'd spread into a patch. Dean and Cal set me up and trusted I would learn. It was one of the best gifts anyone ever gave me.

I didn't know I cared about gardening until I dug my hands in. I'd had no inkling of how hard I would fall for the seemingly repetitive and menial tasks required of the job. I would never have guessed that coaxing a seedling into ornate life could be so tactile, so intimate. Gardening helped me take everything more slowly. It helped me to see deeper down. It squared me with where I come from and with my current place in the world. And it gave me, simultaneously, a chance to be the queen of my own little domain, while also leaving me thrillingly open to the whims of wild chance. Sometimes I'd plant a columbine and the nasturtium would take hold instead. Sometimes a volunteer tomato plant ended up being the best producer of the season. And sometimes I went out to pick kale, only to discover the backside of every leaf encrusted in gray aphids resembling sesame seeds.

I had never before felt a real connection to the land—or specifically, the everyday earth under my shoes. Dirt was a blank substance—it was neutral to me, of no consequence. I had no knowledge of the range of life it contains. I had subconsciously shrugged off the places in which I had lived, believing them to be subpar right down to their dull and depleted soil. It had always taken a trip to a far-flung, beautiful place to elicit wide-eyed terrestrial appreciation in me, but when I began to plant a native garden and grow vegetables, I gave that view up. There would be enough here to entertain me. Rather than always looking toward the big, sweeping things, I began to gaze straight into the ground.

Angelo and Fiorella took avid notice that we'd been steadily improving the lot since moving in; I imagine this was our saving grace in their eyes, because inside the house we were loud, we stayed up late, and we listened to weird music. Angelo and I began to have quick but regular chats through the tall wooden fence that separated our yards, his little dog skittering and barking and licking my hands. One day, when the landscaping was looking particularly orderly, Angelo yelled sweetly over the fence, competing with his Sinatra on the AM radio, "It looks-a like a villa ovah there!"

I could see that their garden would forever kick my garden's ass in terms of productivity—they had it rigged for maximum efficiency and used whatever they could put their hands on as planters—recycling bins, old bathtubs, trash cans. Their enormous grape arbor sent vines over my side of the fence, the leaves cascading prettily in lush layers. In late summer, the mellow scent of Concord grapes drifted across the grass. Angelo stood on the other side, smoking, coughing. I thought of his white hair, the way it sat vulnerably against the deeply tanned skin of his neck.

Angelo's tendency to mumble was so ingrained that there were often long strings of words and deep swings in intonation from which I could glean no more than a word or two. He mixed in Italian phrases when the English equivalent didn't come to him in time. But I learned the patterns of his speech, and how he formed certain words, and soon enough I was able to respond with something more apropos than a nervous laugh or a blank nod. The tone of our conversations was world-weary, put-upon, as if we both had a thankless and impossible job to get done. He'd complain a little about his health, his medications, his tomato yield; I'd complain a little about the rats, litter, and my uncontrollable cucumber vines. Under the grousing, we were communicating our love and admiration for one another. He was an older and traditional man, and I was a younger, unmarried woman with a host of unfamiliar characters visiting my house at all hours. He probably found the whole situation a little strange, but he never let on. He was happy that the house and garden were in somewhat stable hands, because you never know around here.

We began to trade our wares. I gave him jars of the jam that I made every year from his grapes. And he handed me fat glowing tomatoes over the fence and pushed basil seedlings on me whether I had room in the garden or not. I passed them baskets of strawberries, and they tossed me escarole and arugula. "You gotta wash that scarola," Fiorella would caution me, as if the dirt still clinging to its core necessitated an apology. Fiorella once asked me if I had grandparents; I said they'd all passed away long ago. She gave me a rough squeeze and said, "*We're* your grandparents now!" I was shocked, fortified, a little in love. No one passing by would have known we were here, side by side, tucked behind our defeated, old houses, on green and flowering concrete plots.

Before I could relax and enjoy our swish new backyard, there was one more big project that couldn't wait: our mess of a bathroom. This room epitomized the lazy and cheap renovations Al had put in place, which we'd been deliberately trying to wipe away since we'd moved in. I called a contractor friend, Shawn, and we worked out a time frame. James, Shawn, and I demo'd the old bathroom, throwing dried-out pieces of plaster and wood from the third-floor window and exultantly watching them slam to the ground below. Shawn spent a good month of his life in this unventilated, ultra-dusty, sweltering shell of a room, putting up new drywall, knocking out a wall in order to swap out the summer camp shower stall with a proper bathtub/shower, replacing the vinyl floor with smooth bamboo, switching the sad little sink out with a basic but comparatively luxurious Ikea model that could accommodate facewashing, and—vitally—removing the door from the next room over, while covering over the resulting hole with drywall. He also added built-in bookshelves to that room, which helped me justify my book habit. In one fell swoop, Shawn—a stickler who took his time and did it right—removed many of the irritants that plagued me in this apartment, and applied a salve to the burn in the form of things that worked as they should, didn't look ridiculous, and fit in the space provided.

This house was starting to come together.

Itching for another summer of restrained flirtation with Nick, but knowing I should be good, I readied myself to weather another Fourth of July. This time, James and I had the wherewithal to know that staying in the neighborhood would only infuriate us. Avoiding the heat and the noise became job number one. Escaping just as the blasts started up, we drove south to the Wood River, near the town he grew up in, and rented a canoe for the day. It felt luxurious to be surrounded by sounds of nature, by rushing water instead of crackling explosives. We tossed a bag of pretzels and a few cans of seltzer and beer into the canoe, and pushed off. We paddled, we stopped for a swim, we paddled, we swam some more. The sun came through the leaves; the bugs zipped in a cloud that clipped the surface of the river.

We got along that day, but there was always a hard edge to our togetherness. Our fun was usually centered on mocking things, judging people, with a negative current to it even in the best of times. It had become clear that we both believed we were ignoring an essential part of ourselves by being together. By now I was neither attracted to James nor willing to accept that he wasn't attracted to me. I tried to picture him before he let his gray hair grow to the middle of his back, and before his beard concealed his thin face, but the vision was obscured. Then I pictured Nick, new and untarnished in my mind, someone who was fresh and funny, who didn't obliquely hate me, and whose mind wasn't 100 percent decided on every topic in existence. But I did nothing. I stayed unhappy; I told no one how unhappy I was. I acted like a happy person. I'd never met anyone else like James, and I mistook that for a reason to stay in a relationship with him, and not simply to be happy to know him.

To break up is to be a mover, and I am a stayer.

As Nick and I became good friends, I watched him date a few ladies and made note of his love interests.

They were rowdier than me, unpredictable and flagrantly sexy, less apt to give a fuck. They were cool; they were intimidating—the kind of women of whom I'd already been jealous my whole life. Wildness could get you in trouble, but so could cautiousness.

Nick would give me some little bit of detail on a misstep he'd made with a woman he'd been dating, and—having been let in on his inner workings, the curtain concealing his dating rationale drawn back—my white-hot attraction began to simmer down to an inconspicuous flicker. I wish I could say that we once made out ferociously while James was in the next room, but I never gave Nick any sign of my crush. Because I'm both a champion hider of love interest and in possession of a tone-deaf obliviousness to others' interest in me, I have absolutely no idea if he returned my admiration. I know he observed my relationship with James and saw that it was rather flimsy in spots.

As his time in the house lengthened, I started to think of Nick as a brother-in-arms, someone who believed as much as I did that we could make this a dream living situation, a punk house with a heart. Although that goal may have been a touch too lofty, he was the person who made it seem noble, a worthwhile place to find ourselves.

During Nick's stay, we were tormented by the presence of a group of very active drug dealers who operated from the second floor of the house directly across the street, a triple-decker like mine, its vinyl siding once white but now a crusty gray. There was no specific offending event—it just sucks to live near a crack house, and to know that you live near a crack house. The house always looked cold and bereft. The lights were usually kept off. The door stayed unlocked all day and night, banging open in the wind, even in winter. Cars pulled up, cars pulled away. The clientele hassled my tenants and me on the street. There was a mundane gloominess to it all.

Annoyed, my neighbors and I steeled ourselves to outlast the problem. We traded acerbic comments about firebombing the place. One winter morning, after years of indignantly observing the house for sport, I spent a happy hour or so sipping coffee and watching from the third floor of my house as a bunch of FBI agents in bulletproof vests raided the house. People were arrested, the house vacated. It sat hauntingly empty for months, its rammed-in front door like a black eye as it slept off the comedown. When it sold to a new owner, a crew came around and did some mild sprucing, painting and replacing the busted front door.

The house has since been home to a succession of nice people: single moms and their kids, students, twentysomethings with Obama signs in their windows. But it's hard for me to see this particular house anew. My eyes still slip right back to its broken past. Realizing this has lightened my judgment of the neighborhood's old guard, the few Italian American families who stuck around Federal Hill until the present, who never left for the suburbs, the stubborn ones who continue to cling to vestiges of sameness and ritual. They're no longer the majority; they feel threatened; a toxic bitterness leeches from some of them. In situations where I've been forced to confront these people, I'm put off by their fear of the future. But being privy to the crack house in full swing, and then watching the ravaged shell sit in its aftermath, I've become aware that my inclinations toward this one house may be like the inclinations of the old guard toward the entire neighborhood. Where I saw one house in decline and decay, they see an entire neighborhood comprised of old housing that has fallen into disrepair, and yeah, that is sad. But I don't blame the current mix of renters and owners within those homes for the waning grandeur of the neighborhood—especially not on the basis of their race, ethnicity, or socioeconomic standing. I suspect that the old guard might.

A friend and coffee shop coworker of mine mentioned that she needed a place to stay for a couple of months while her girlfriend looked for an apartment in Washington, DC, where they planned to move. I was psyched and quickly offered her the "extra" room in our apartment—as extra as a room can be when one's living space is eight hundred square feet—for a couple hundred bucks a month. Amanda brought a mattress, some clothes, and her bike, and we settled in to shit-talk our way through the rest of the season of *Project Runway*. She and I sat at the kitchen table making up new words* and a variety of memes involving my oversized cat, Kernel.

Her girlfriend Kelly stayed with us, too, when she was back in town.

It was crowded, but in a madcap way, the women chattering away, unleashing unimaginable amounts of sarcasm and outtalking the normally long-winded James. Then, James's twenty-year-old goth metal-loving nephew, Adam, decided to come to Providence from a foreclosure-ridden manufactured community in Florida, where he'd been living with his dad. He was experiencing the type of misery you would expect from a darkness-embracing kid living in a sunny Southern suburb, and we worried about his fate should he not get out immediately. So he too showed up at PennHenge with little warning. Adam's favorite uncle James acted as his oddball mentor and creative coach. We had no more extra rooms, so Adam got the couch. I was game—I wanted to help this sad, broke boy—but I was in denial about the loss of the couch I so enjoyed. With this one last addition, we seemed to cross a line into sitcom territory: a frustrated straight couple, a chatty lesbian couple, two ill-behaved male cats, and a young mall goth who drew on his face every day with black Sharpie, all in one two-bedroom apartment.

Meanwhile, the persistent need for regular money and health insurance swung me back in the direction of the nine-to-five world, and I'd accepted a

---

*Our best work was *nauticrap* (n): A subcategory of pricey antiques salvaged from ships or other seafaring vessels, i.e., buoys, anchors, mastheads, knotwork, scrimshaw, etc.

full-time job as an editor at a small audiobook publisher. I was starting up a new publishing division;
not only did I not know how to do that, my bosses didn't either, so there was a lot of nebulous, on-
the-fly decision-making that left me flustered and
exhausted. By the time I got home at night, I just
wanted mindless quiet. I wanted my apartment
back. The overcrowding had been livable at first, but
at some point I noticed each of us had locked ourselves into whichever room we could be alone. This
made it a challenge to get into the bathroom, the one
room I needed unfettered access to at all times. My
digestive worries were somehow growing still worse,
and more painful, no matter how much doctor-
sanctioned fiber I ritualistically put into my face.

Amanda and Kelly left town as planned. And it
turned out that James's persistent life instruction
was transformative, because soon Adam found a
job, and then an apartment. By then interaction between Adam and me had dwindled to a floor-gazing
near-silence.

With everyone safely on their respective ways,
PennHenge enjoyed a short few weeks of peace. But
soon the tension was running hot once again. Nick
had decided to move out. He wasn't getting along
with Dean; their friendship had melted down under the pressure of living together, and with Cal
a constant presence. Cal and Dean weren't getting
along, either. I stayed especially far afield of the
conflict, being that I loved all three of these people.
My knowing the details would only serve to lessen
my impartiality. Staying in the dark also helped

me hang on to the overly hopeful notion that this would easily blow over in record time. To nurture an atmosphere of reconciliation, I walked on tiptoe, turned down the stereo, burned incense, and napped a lot. I sought to keep the PennHenge environs aggressively happy; I hoped my calm vibes could somehow diminish the conflict, and get everybody to hug and forget about it.

Despite the recent trouble between them, Dean and Cal were an endearing pairing. They worked together, in the warm air, their hands in the lush soil and the breeze ruffling their hair. They made their own schedules, and they grew and sold their own food. They cooked feasts; they played music. A pure air of self-determination seemed to permeate both of them. In my confusion and weakness, my own relationship a sham, having returned to work in a beige office behind a beige desk and feeling the eternal hankering for fresh air and freedom, I gazed at them as if they held ancient knowledge, some secret to a meaningful life that I could look in on.

In a sense, they did help me find my way. But they were as conflicted as anyone else.

Nick left, and all was strangely quiet. I missed his grounding presence.

All of my tiptoeing around and providing a healing atmosphere may as well have been directed right back at me, considering the state of my relationship. I'd been thinking about how I was going to break up with James for months. We'd accomplished a lot together, but any foundation of love and trust we thought we'd built was imaginary. I was overrun with resentment toward him, unable to react to his everyday trials with compassion because he owed me emotional and financial debts we both knew he'd never repay. I felt belittled, lonely, and alienated. Buying and maintaining the house while working a full-time job had required a lot of dull sacrifices, and I felt ashamed because he intimated that I wasn't doing enough creative shit. I didn't think he appreciated all I had done to get us this house—at *his* urging—while he continued in much the same way as before, feeling little of the stress of owning Penn-Henge. I was irritated with him for expecting me to pay his way, and with myself for paying it.

I was attached to him, but I couldn't remember why. I was still trying to fulfill the role of long-suffering girlfriend, grasping at anything that might pass for love. We were together because we'd been together. We hadn't kissed in years.

He felt it too—he was charting the end of the voyage. That was exactly what he was aiming for when he took off from a party with a young art student, coming home supremely haggard in the morning. That evening, I (shamefully) read his Facebook messages. The talk was of how drunk they'd been, but still they'd managed to fuck, haha! I stomped into the bedroom, where James was napping, calling him a selfish asshole, telling him he needed to leave. He had little to say, but at least he didn't deny it. I was pissed off. I was relieved.

It took a couple of ugly days, but we quickly and cleanly ended our nearly nine-year relationship. He felt terrible, which was the right thing, but in his remorse I sensed a paternalistic quality—like he felt he had done a bad job at protecting me, the precious flower, the weak little woman. This was so far from how I saw myself that I wanted to scream in his face, beat his chest, let him know that there were many definitions of strength and that mine had carried us both for years.

We'd lived at PennHenge together for nearly three years. The relationship was mourned before it was over—I'd already visualized it so thoroughly. I was thirty years old. I was single, lonely, and in no hurry to fulfill any biological destiny. I was going to find out what it meant to live alone.

It could be said that James stuck me with the largest, most glaring piece of relationship baggage imaginable, a monstrous actualization of the hopelessness of our entanglement. He pushed me to buy this demanding house, in effect hastening our demise, and took off to start fresh and free elsewhere. Immediately post-breakup, when I *wanted* to be angry, maybe I played that card. But in actuality, I was grateful for the house. It offered me continuity and dependability (though it was often dependably insane). I didn't have to uproot myself entirely to end this relationship. I was suddenly free to make the house fully mine, without towing anybody along. I'm glad I got the chance to say "Get your stuff and get the fuck out of my house" once in my life. Every long-suffering girlfriend deserves to utter those words.

Couples, Retreat

Starting out, I thought I was going to be the Mama Bear, the matriarch of a hassle-free empire of lovers and thinkers. Cheap rent for good people. I pictured an atmosphere heavy on kitsch, chickpeas, art, and greenery; with good friends always around; and tenants popping upstairs to say hi. I would cook hippie-food dinners for everyone, and we'd all digest our food sitting on the floor in my living room, playing music and making each other laugh. I'd be at the center, smiling beatifically at my charges. *Why cloister myself in a single-family house,* I thought, *when I can have a wild bunch of friends around 24/7?*

Oh, but the wildness was only beginning. It just didn't take the form I'd planned.

A few months after the drama on the second floor between Nick and Dean, and not long after James and I broke up, Dean and Cal's relationship also imploded. It just happened to occur around the same time that, on the first floor, Caroline and Elvin were breaking up. Living with so much emotional wreckage lent an apocalyptic air of stern mourning to the house. The postmortem plans were thus: Dean would move out; Cal would share the apartment with her good pal, bandmate, and fellow recently single lady

Caroline, who was adamant about staying at Penn-Henge. There was just one minor flaw here: her grouchy ex Elvin, with whom things were rocky at best, would be living directly below her. It was delusional to think this plan could work, but there were so many delicate egos in the house at that moment that it had to be sorted a bit at a time.

I began to think of the place as "The House That Kills Love." Love among weirdos is famously hard to maintain, but man, we were running up a karmic tab with all of these long-term relationship deaths on the premises. Romances that seemed downright robust at the time of move-in crumbled under the roof of this portentous palace. In strifey times, a particular weighty silence pervades the house, subtly signaling that another bond is being broken. I hold my breath, waiting for the unmistakable relationship death throes to make themselves heard. Voices raised, then hushed; doors slamming; huffy, late-night leaving, then returning in sobs; drunken crying; full-bore yelling, every word totally intelligible throughout the quiet house. A chilly emotional wind is blowing through, brushing up against everyone at PennHenge. A pervasive communal shiver ruffles through us all.

Once dead at last, the relationship detangling begins in earnest. Who will move out? Will anyone stay? Who gets to keep all the best records? Who gets to keep the couch? What happens to the cat? It's inhumane to have to consider such things when in the midst of an emotional catastrophe. The home base becomes the seat of relationship mourning, the place where all objects, seasons, and fleeting feelings remind the mourner of what she had, and how she has fucked it up. It's hard to be there; it's hard to leave.

Amid dreadful, protracted screamfests with Elvin, Caroline had been living upstairs for a month or so when Cal—also cracking under interrelated stresses—moved out and returned to Baltimore practically unannounced. Determined, Caroline found yet another roommate—a real feat considering her precarious emotional state. We all hoped Elvin would tire of this arrangement and move out, but he was entrenched by then, harnessing a spiteful fortitude to outlast her. After a few contentious months, she conceded. The opportunistic nature of the situation was the kicker—either of them could flip at any moment, and the object of their frustration was always close enough to casually eviscerate. This could not go on indeterminately. Embattled, Caroline and her roommate again packed up their things and moved to another house in another part of town, one where drama wasn't assumed, and the walls weren't painted in sad.

Really, though, *is* there something in the walls here? In the pipes? Some jilted spirit that demands a reckoning? Perhaps a bad energy that I need to cleanse? Friends have suggested burning sage and performing healing chants.

The grand, operatic drama of synchronized relationship meltdowns and apartment scrambling was over, but it had exacted a toll on all of us. The tension subsided, and within a few weeks it no longer felt as if the roof was going to blow off volcano-style.

There was relief in knowing that these great ladies could now move on sans male encumbrances, but I missed perching on the stoop talking about life stuff with Cal or posting up in the garage on a rainy night with Caroline, smoking and polishing off a cheap jug of wine. From this point forward, with few exceptions, my tenants would all be men.

Having women in the house made the place feel more looked after, and it was dreamy to be mere seconds from an impromptu hang at all times. Being in each other's space gave our relationships an immediacy, a real-time understanding of one another. We looked at each other and recognized the fight; we wordlessly agreed to support one another. Even toward the end of their stay, when these women were feeling out of control, when the high drama was at its climax, they kept it together. We treated each other with sweetness and caring. They respected me and the house, and—not to be taken for granted— made it smell really nice. They told me how much they loved living here and didn't want to leave. But circumstances made them leave anyway.

When I later ran into any of the inhabitants from the PennHenge Couples Meltdown period, they usually avoided looking at me directly. They were uneasy. Perhaps I was a representative of a bad place, a portal to bad times, and to look at me meant acknowledging that the place still existed, somewhat unchanged, with me sitting tattered at the unhealthy helm. That old shiver floods back with one look at my face.

Caroline later admitted that she was pissed at me

for a while after she left because I didn't stand up for her strongly enough when things with Elvin were boiling over. She was right. I took the path of least resistance, reluctant to step into the conflict; instead of telling Elvin to go, I let them work it out for themselves—which did not produce an amicable solution, but rather scarred Caroline in ways that I now know took her years to heal. I wish I could take that back; I wish I could have nurtured Caroline at that time, instead of deflecting involvement. Frankly, I was intimidated by Elvin's anger—gleaming, sharp, and omnipresent as it was back then—I thought he'd hurt me too.

This period of breakups and apartment shuffling may have been the moment when my idealistic desire to install a harmonious group of lovers and thinkers under my roof began to slip from view, engulfed as it was by the pressures of staving off said lovers' and thinkers' emotional disasters. I began to think maybe just paying the mortgage and keeping the rooms occupied was enough of a challenge.

I was drained from seeking good people out, inviting them in, and then watching them leave. My level of caring notched slightly down; I was tired of letting the house dominate my thoughts, and in my fatigue I thought leaving it all up to chance might work as well as controlling every detail. We were sliding backward into what I justified was a more businesslike arrangement: from "friends who live in the same house" to straight-up tenants and landlady. You pay me, you live here. Simple and sucky PennHcnge was once comprised of people with lots in common, who happened to live together; now I was flipping that dynamic on its head, setting up a zone where people lived together, and had little in common.

But this was a risky move, for my own psyche had by now become intertwined with PennHenge such that when the house or its occupants were unwell, so was I. Being nice and making sure the heat stayed on seemed somehow too basic. I still hankered for the close bonds that had been so slippery throughout this experience. Do other landlords feel this way, I wondered? Do they fret over their houses as if they're troubled children, loved but in danger?

I suppose the house *is* my dependent. In a way— and arbitrary as such things are—it's the only badge identifying me as an adult.

Elvin brought in his friend Johnny, a metalhead body piercer, as his new, post-breakup roommate. Johnny had a young daughter who would stay with us for a day or two at a time. Being heavily pierced, pale, hangdog, and clothed entirely in black, Johnny looked hardened and unfriendly. He seemed tested to the limit by his own existence, his persona a bald statement of negativism. He didn't say a whole lot, and he wasn't exactly a barrel of laughs, but when we did talk, I always felt that he ran deep, and that he cared. He'd admire the garden and we'd talk about his family, his daughter, his job, and mine too. I worked hard to get a laugh out of him; each time he huffed out a quick, staccato cackle, I felt a glimmer arise from him.

Between Johnny and Elvin, the first floor was

morphing into a nihilist bachelor pad. Caroline's cheeky decorative touches were slowly wiped from the apartment; the general feel of the place became darker and dirtier as the windows were covered with thick cloth, such was the boys' aversion to natural light. A thick wall of sludgy guitar blasted forth from the stereo. They never cooked; they didn't clean. I imagined Johnny's daughter sitting among a pile of beer bottles and pizza boxes, waiting for their weekly outdoor time: "Dad, can we go now?"

Upstairs from Elvin and Johnny, the second floor was newly empty. I did some small-time work on the place—painting and macrolevel cleaning and putting new knobs on drawers. But there was no rent coming in, and being responsible for this extra share of the mortgage meant I was *bur-roke*. I made the friend rounds, trying to be relaxed about scaring up new tenants, but interest was low and leases unable to be broken. The spectacle of recent relationship failures in every corner of the house had roundly defeated me, and I was not entirely competent to seek emotionally healthy, new second-floor tenants. I was frustrated, a touch desperate, and maybe a little bit in the mood to fuck things up. From this crumbling ledge, I stepped off into a blinding wind of unsound tenants.

But it was also glorious summer in Rhode Island, and I was a few weeks into dating someone new. I'd seen Seth at an art opening and made a shameless beeline for him. This behavior was way out of my norm, but I saw him sitting by himself, sipping a drink in a butter-yellow sweater, and my feet sort of moved themselves. I saw him again a few weeks later, at a show, and the same thing happened.

Seth was a very talented audio engineer, a thoughtful, funny guy, a loyal friend, and someone who could effortlessly make any location or situation fun. He worked for an old friend of mine, so I slid right back in with his familiar crowd. Seth and I lolled around on the beach, went to the movies, sang giddily along to every song on the radio, laughed constantly. It was a connection forged in fun, so different from the one I'd shared with James, which had been forged in intensity and suffering in the months after his dad passed away.

I wanted to be around Seth as much as possible, and he clearly felt the same way, but we played it cool because I was only a few months out of that nearly nine-year thing with James. At thirty to his twenty-one, I was also nine years older than Seth—somebody prepare the numerology charts—which one minute seemed crucially ominous and the next like a nonissue. Seth was short, skinny, and scruffy and wore holey jeans and threadbare T-shirts; being roughly the same size, we traded clothes.

Seth's life revolved around music, both because his curiosity for it was so intense, and also because his job was strangely 24/7. Although a lot of the music he recorded was intentionally difficult, sloppy, or impenetrable, his own understanding of music was clean and precise. He rarely got a day off; he enjoyed being needed at work, being "the only one" who could fix a problem or be on call for one thing or another.

But he was graced with a day off on the Fourth

of July, and we traded texts with barely concealed excitement. I was delirious, eager to spend the day with him, but I wasn't sure whether our relationship standing yet included hanging out on holidays. He texted to suggest a bike ride from Providence to the seaside town he grew up in, where we'd hang out with his family, watch a parade, have a cookout, drink American amounts of alcohol. Shocked by this seeming early admission of heavy interest on his part, I was all in. Any mainstream women's magazine in existence would confer grave importance to my having been asked to meet the family, but our relationship was only three weeks and a handful of dates old. In this act, he was bringing me closer, yes, but not because he gave credence to any of the traditional milestones of dating. He was neither a player of games nor an assigner of meaning, not that I quite knew that yet. I *did* know that if there was one thing I was down to do, it was to jump into something messy and poorly defined and full of cloaked passion. I'd been love-starved for years.

Getting on our bikes a bit late, in danger of missing the parade, caffeinated but with no food in our bellies, improperly attired, and not in possession of even a bottle of water, Seth suggested that we make up for lost time by biking faster than usual. I spent the hour-and-a-half ride out of breath, my legs on fire, trying to catch his jean-clad ass as it continually disappeared on the bike path ahead of me. This would become a metaphor for our relationship: he moved so fast; he couldn't be still; he sometimes willingly vanished from my horizon.

When we arrived at his parents' house, I was red and hyperventilating, sweating beyond the heat, unable to push the pedals even one more time around. My guts flailed. But I loved his parents instantly; warm, funny, reliable, doting, and still clearly in love, they welcomed me. His mom cracked witticisms about her casual garb for the day ("this is *my* Independence Day, Vikki!"); his studious yet rugged dad threw the Frisbee for the dog. I felt instantly included in the family, let in on all the jokes, part of a united front fortified by potato salad and hummus. Getting a ride with Seth's dad back to the city, resting in the backseat of their Subaru wagon, having spent a sun-soaked day eating, kayaking, swimming, and walking the dog around their suburban neighborhood in its silly, patriotic revelry, I was giddy. These beautiful people had raised this sweet man. It felt like every force—internal and external—was propelling me toward him.

As I floated deeper into the reverie, I had to come up for air at least long enough to half-assedly rent out the second-floor apartment, which had now been empty for a couple of months. Through a friend of a friend, a solution came in the form of a turtle-faced guy with the intriguing nickname of Dougie Peppers, who worked at an upscale grocery and seemed, if not charming, at least stable enough. But stories started percolating my way—immediately *after* he moved in—alluding that he owed more money and had stolen more stuff from my friends around town than could possibly be coincidental. Yeah, he seemed kind of squirrely, for sure, but I wasn't going to fall for the small-town scuttlebutt without giving him a chance.

He started out with one roommate, a rangy, spacey, tweaked redhead punker named Cheryl, but within weeks he was moving other friends in (without asking or even informing me) so he could get help in paying the rent. As one new recruit would prove unable to cough up cash—or unable to handle the personalities involved—another would take his place. There were three new arrivals in rapid succession. The third one was a charmer I dubbed Stoner Joe—part hippie, part raver, part sleazeball, part acid casualty, part rap-rock Jesse Pinkman, he was an intoxicating mix. The instant I laid eyes on Joe, I felt a strong urge to change the locks on the doors. He always looked to be on the verge of a meltdown or a bender. He had a talent for saying the creepiest thing at the moment you turned away, when you thought you were done talking with him. I would sneak out to work in the garden, hoping to evade him, but he would come outside shirtless and stretch out in a lawn chair with a bong, sighing into the sunlight, vaguely hitting on me, and chugging beer. He brought home an abandoned pit bull, which humanized him a bit but added stress to the house as the untrained dog barreled through, barking and jumping on people, Joe making no move to calm him down.

This crew was loud, drunk, petty, and fiery. They fought like siblings, in a whiny fashion, constantly.

They seemed unable to stay out of one another's hair, unable to understand the concept of a peaceful existence. The tension was way up and the drugs were being doled out at frequent intervals.

Stoner Joe, Dougie Peppers, and Cheryl were often unable to pay the $700 rent in full. Sometimes, they'd pay half of it; sometimes, they'd pay two-thirds. It was difficult to impress upon them that the monthly rent amount was not merely a suggested retail price but rather a contract with which they were bound to comply. I uneasily bugged them for money every month, stressing one moment about asking them and the next about not being able to pay the bills. I didn't like these people as human beings—and as tenants, they were beyond the pale. It was soul-crushing to endure even a one-minute conversation with them.

Seth wanted little to do with PennHenge. This wasn't a particularly illustrious time in its tenure, so I couldn't take much issue there. Even I wasn't jumping at the chance to be affiliated with it. I remember his reaction upon walking into my apartment for the first time: unimpressed. "Charming but off-kilter" didn't do it for him; he preferred precise and sleek, the same way he did his job. Of the newly renovated bathroom, he backhanded, "It's the nicest room in the house."

Although he was now very clearly my full-fledged boyfriend, there was no doubt that I was still going it alone. I hesitated to ask him to invest his brainpower or ultra-limited free time to help me with some house chore. I thought he might see such a request as a drag on our fun. I daydreamed that in a year or two he might want to move in with me, but even as I considered it, I felt him hoping I would never ask. His lack of interest hurt a little because my house was an extension of me—including (and especially) the unkempt parts. But I didn't buy the house with Seth, I told myself, so he was under no obligation to spend his rare nights off helping me nail trim into the window frames. He did his best to contribute, but even an unusually stable twenty-two-year-old man has limited tolerance for old-house problems.

I reasoned: *If he loves me but doesn't love my house, we can find a work-around.* I tabled the thought, knowing it was too early in the game to be strategizing in that direction.

Gathering up whatever toughness resided in me, I eventually had to boot out the Dougie Peppers/Cheryl/Stoner Joe trifecta. I was horrified to have to be the enforcer, but the situation was past the point of reason. These guys were a festering mess, and every day they stuck around, the stain sunk deeper in. I had to preserve my self-respect. If I didn't do it soon, they'd only get more entrenched, which meant they'd break more beer bottles, yell more, not pay the rent more, act like petulant assholes more.

After several minutes of deep-breathing exercises, I knocked on their door, my breath shallow. Cheryl opened it. I clenched my fists by my sides and opened my mouth to speak. As I did, she preempted with, "We're movin' out. We'll be out in a week. Is that what you were coming to ask?" I stuttered back at her that yes, that was it, and actually *thanked her*—because god, it was such a relief to have it over with, no screaming, no fighting, no threats. I kicked into gear, said something like, "Yeah, thank you, please leave now; I'd really appreciate it." I almost felt badly that it had gone so smoothly. And they did go away as scheduled, leaving me to that same old dilemma: empty apartment, insufficient income, and lack of exceptional examples of humanity clamoring to be part of my life experiment.

When the second floor was again empty, I did a new round of cleaning and painting. Windows open, spirits chased out, hot water, soap, mops, the whole bit. These people didn't have much stuff that couldn't be jammed into milk crates, so they didn't really leave anything behind—just a few scratched records and a lone, crusty crack pipe hanging out on a shelf in the closet.

Loneliness is sometimes recognizable only in retrospect. In the day-to-day, there is stuff to do, so much busyness masquerading as fulfillment, such that you may not notice the cracking of your mental terrain. Someone I love once told me that I like adversity—which seems like a really self-important thing to repeat to you now, but in the context of this person's comment, it was meant in a literal sense that I do not like the way to be too easy. If I have the choice to walk somewhere or to drive a car, I will always walk. If it starts pouring while I'm on my bike, I take it as a fun novelty. If I get lost in the woods at sundown, a little thrill runs through me. So, maybe I enjoyed the adversity of living with difficult people and of seeking devotion from a man who, when pressed, told me he cared about me, but never that he loved me. Someone with whom I could get a month deep and stay there for years, trying to coax more out of it, bumping up against the end of it again and again.

Title T. P.

I am not proud to inform you that I once sent this text message, verbatim, to my tenants: **Dudes. Please don't flush anything other than poo, pee, and toilet paper. Line will get blocked again. Thanks bros!**

I trotted out this memorandum—mortifying on so many levels—after a messy sewage backup situation that allowed me to meet several new repairmen. It cost $667; it was dirty, infectious, and aromatic. So, despite my discomfort, I had to let my tenants know that it must not happen again. Dementedly punching out this text, I laughed to myself: I would send them something so embarrassing and impolite that they would heretofore treat the plumbing with extreme respect, if only to have me never discuss their toilet habits ever again.

Living with tenants is about facing their emotional upheavals, their hygienic idiosyncrasies, their fetishes and pet peeves, their tastes and volume preferences in music, all of it. Sometimes down to the level of telling people explicitly what can be placed in a toilet.

Rather than doing the sensible thing, i.e., renting the apartments in my home to quiet, pleasant, law-abiding working folk who turn in early and don't make trouble, I've chosen to live with an unpredictable but entertaining mix of lovable freaks. It really ups the potential for human and financial calamity, but it's how I've always chosen to roll. My tendency toward trusting people is a bit bruised, but remains largely intact. I'm aware that most people are unbearable and some are routinely evil. I just keep believing that the good ones will somehow find their way to me.

After several years of haphazardly running the show at PennHenge, I ran into a friend who had just bought a two-family house in town. I congratulated her, welcoming her to the landlady club. We commiserated for a hot minute, and in doing so, she made a few offhand comments like, "When I was checking my tenant's credit . . ." or "On his rental application he wrote . . ." I nodded along, like, of course, references and credit checks and applications, yep, ha, the tools of the trade, right? Meanwhile, I was mortified that I'd *never* done any of these things. I'd been speeding ahead just assuming things would work out, while everybody else had been exercising their due diligence.

I can't pin my tendency to dodge standard protocols entirely on my Gen X birth year, but I can say that I was irreversibly affected by the cheeky slacker mentality that prevailed during my teenage years. Music was the trigger; music showed me both a level of sensory depth that I hadn't yet been exposed to and approaches to life that were unlike my tidy small-town existence. Getting into punk and post punk in the nineties—Fugazi and Pavement and

P. J. Harvey and Sonic Youth—and observing the witty side-eye these performers squinted at society was a potent signal; I picked it up hungrily. It pointed the way for me at that skeptical national moment in time. Sure, they all sold records, but these bands were just as interested in unifying people, in working within a meaningful scene. They toured like maniacs, often hitting the small cities like Providence; my friends and I lobbied our parents for ticket money for months ahead of the shows.

Their influence decisively changed my friends and me. They made us willing to proudly step out of line.

The thrill of going to a record store to pick up a brand-new LP by a band you'd discovered—having maybe heard one track from it if you were lucky enough to catch it on college radio—was pure, always new. Selecting one from a fresh stack, weighing the thing (bound pleasingly in shrink wrap), reading the track names, tucking it under your arm, then plunking down the fifteen bucks you'd saved up, nodding to the counter dude: heavenly.

You were taking a chance; you couldn't stream it on Spotify. You had to go home and cross your fingers as you put the needle into the groove.

You could not Instagram your purchase. You could not buy it on Amazon.

The time before the internet is hard to recall, but when I get a clear moment of it, I feel like I'm gazing at a slow, pink sunset. It's that light that everyone looks good in.

In my teens, I became smart and cynical; I objected to conspicuous consumption and barcodes and being marketed to. Among my crowd, "selling out"—making art or music that appealed to the masses, that could make money—was an unforgivable sin. I've been trying to get out from underneath my seesawing slacker-versus-overachiever expectations ever since. Buying PennHenge and selecting a long line of opinionated outsiders to live in it with me has added up to a series of proclamations: I'm tough and capable, and nobody can tell me how to live; I want to be with my weirdo brethren; we spit on your plywood mansion out in the suburbs. Even when none of the above is particularly true—when the experience of owning the house is terrible and I've stopped wholly believing in it—even then, I'm happy it's not ordinary.

So the framework I've built my tenant relationships on is convoluted. It's not predicated, as most are, on the simple exchange of money for space. In my mind at least, we're all on a loose but spirited mission together, united by our tendency to resist blending in with the pack. Therefore, I hate to chastise my tenants, even when they act like boneheads. I don't raise their rent. There's a silent agreement on all sides to live and let live.

Still, I am the (female) quasi-authority figure in a house full of males who dislike authority. Conflicts rear up, and somebody has to deal with them. I thus maintain an air of nonconfrontational, jocular innocence 90 percent of the time, with 10 percent mild toughness thrown in when warranted. This carefully calibrated elixir works sufficiently most of the timo, but when it fails, it fails hard.

That's because you cannot predict how the tenant-landlord relationship will evolve once the wheels get to turning—once *theoretically* sharing a house becomes *actually* seeing each other in the hall in various states of undress. Invariably, we start out with pleasantries, as everybody puts their best foot forward, striving with every shred of their being to seem nice, normal, and responsible. With some people, that lasts just until the final box is moved in, and then they career immediately off the tracks.

When someone doesn't like living here, I sense it quickly. When things aren't working out with a tenant, the house is hollow. And then there are the ones who are completely willing to destroy you and your home if you let them in. The exemplar of such erratic behavior, the gold star Most Shitty Award winner, and the tenant to whom all others compare favorably, is Neil. I dragged him in during a moment of weakness, and things only got weaker from there.

On a summer afternoon, I drop by a friend's house. There is a skinny, pallid, tattooed, prematurely gray-haired, seemingly jovial dude outside. He's moving stuff out of a beat-up car into his friend's first-floor apartment. I hear him say he's looking for a place in town, hopefully right in the neighborhood. Without a moment's further consideration, I pounce, yelling out maybe a little too eagerly, "HEY! YOU'RE LOOKING FOR AN APARTMENT? I HAVE ONE FOR RENT!"

The dude's head whips around; he grins. We chat for a minute. I evaluate: *Quick and dark sense of humor? Check. Some level of employment? Check.* There's a bit of the witty bastard-slash-asshole in him, but this is a male personality type that I am accustomed to handling. I invite him to come see the place later that day. He shows up holding hands with his ladyfriend, Carrie, who is sweet, funny, and friendly. She doesn't have a job at the moment—they just moved here from the Southwest—but she has three interviews in the coming week. Sensing that she is a stabilizing factor in his life, I'm sold on them. They are sold as well. They agree to move in right away.

Neil and Carrie sign a lease. I self-congratulate—turns out, a touch too early, for a couple of days after they're in, Neil announces that he is unhappy with the bathroom and the kitchen in the apartment; they are too worn and dingy. I agree, but tell him there is very little I can afford to do at the moment, and this relative semigrubbiness is why their apartment is such a bargain. He says he is very interested in doing some renovations. Although he has "super limited" experience, he is excited to learn. He's explicit that the apartment *really* needs to be fixed up in order for him and Carrie to enjoy living here, an opinion he did not voice when they looked at the place. (The rent was seven hundred dollars a month and the space, while not fancy, was at the time certainly habitable, clean-ish, a decent place to live.)

Sniffing a foreboding note in the air, but determined not to let these new recruits slip through my fingers—and also thinking a little renovation wouldn't be the worst thing—I agree to help Neil find an antique clawfoot tub and an old farmhouse sink that we will then put in together. Carrie and I begin combing Craigslist, emailing each other photos of tubs, sinks, chandeliers, and other random furnishings. So far, it's all leisurely. But then the schedule changes. On a whim, Neil gets my sledgehammer out of the basement and destroys and removes the current bathtub from the apartment. Just like that. He figures this will spur us to get things done quickly.

With no place for Neil and Carrie to shower, the tub search is accelerated. For a few days, they shower at the Y or at friends' houses. Inevitably, I feel irrationally guilty and offer them my shower. For another couple of days they appear at my door with towels and toiletries, apologizing, at various times of the day and night.

The two haven't paid their first month's rent in full yet.

It is only too clear that the tension between Neil and Carrie is escalating. He drinks heavily. He is erratic and lashes out at her, while I try to run interference and keep them both pacified with tales of how awesome the apartment is soon going to be. The Craiglist trolls with tubs for sale keep flaking out on us, changing appointment times or flat-out disappearing. I still have foolish illusions of hanging on to these two, of watching them settle in and chill out and stop pushing the stress meter into the red zone. But then Neil gets pissy with me, red-faced bitching me out because he's "not seeing the results he expected," and a lengthy email volley begins. At some point I write to Carrie, **Please realize that you guys were the ones who decided to do all of the work you're** doing. I'm perfectly willing to go along with all of it, and pay for it, and I really want you guys to enjoy living in the house, but I didn't actually *ask you* to do anything. And you guys still owe me more than half of the rent for August. Which, again, I'm willing to wait on, but it's not exactly ideal for me, either. Relations are frosty, but Carrie and I make up, rededicating ourselves anew to our shared mission.

Finally, a tub is procured. Neil and a friend-with-truck go and pick it up. I pay for it. It is brought into the apartment and dumped in the living room to await the plumber's arrival. I purchase several hundred dollars–worth of fixtures in order to connect the tub to the plumbing.

Then Carrie breaks up with Neil and moves out, in the space of a single day.

Smart woman. But Neil is wrecked. His self-destructive streak flares. I hear thrashing and crashing downstairs. With her calming presence having split the scene, there's no buffer between him and me, and his testiness, in line with his inebriation, hits new heights. His rage is white-hot and scary. I barely know the guy; I don't know how to react.

A week or so later, Neil calls and informs me that he has lost his job; he cannot pay me the remainder of that month's rent; and he is moving out immediately. I yell at him, via my cell phone from a Home Depot parking lot, in a cathartic, out-of-body style I have never since had reason to employ.

Neil and Carrie's total time in the apartment: just over three weeks.

Neil left a bunch of pitiful stuff behind, and as I

cathartically slipped his stained mattress out of a tall, skinny second-floor window, watching it bounce and land in the street below, I stuck my head out the window and laughed down at it. I'd been so indignant, which suddenly became very funny to me. Taking back Neil's short-lived, soon-to-be-renovated space, felt good too. I turned the process of dumping his garbage and pee-filled beer bottles (Wasn't it the shower that was missing, and not the toilet?) into an only slightly depressing party for one, blasting Kanye, and grinning as I yelled "THAT'S RIGHT, ASSHOLE!" and slammed the lid on the trash can, feeling like I'd mentally hitched a ride on Neil's raging coattails for a bit but could see a way back to being in control again. The adrenaline of taking charge now dazzled my nerve endings. I hoped Carrie was feeling the same way, wherever she was.

At my yearly appointment with the very nice doctor at Planned Parenthood, all seemed to be pretty routine. As a last catch-all question, she asked, "Anything else you want to tell me, just generally?"

It's likely a totally standard question, but it's also possible she saw how pale I was, or the strange hollows of my eyes.

"Uh, I don't think so." Pause. "I mean, I have been kind of tired."

Apparently, "kind of tired," by my definition, was falling asleep repeatedly in the car on my evening commute, then being unable to get out of the car upon pulling into the driveway; I'd recline in the driver's seat and take a half-hour nap right there.

"Kind of tired" was stubbornly insisting on riding my bike, but stopping to cry at the side of the road upon encountering a hill. It was being totally out of breath at the top of the stairs to my apartment. Falling asleep at a very loud show or in a cranked sauna—sometimes standing up.

I'd had my wisdom teeth pulled recently, and the staff at the surgeon's office had "a hard time" bringing me back out from under the anesthesia.

And there was the digestive stuff—which was pretty much ruling my life at this point—but I didn't mention that, because *gross!* and also, she was a gynecologist; she didn't want to know about my rotten intestines.

"Okay, well, let's check your iron levels; maybe that'll give us a clue."

She did the test, left the room to check the results, and came back shaking her head; "That test was faulty," she said, it had given her a funny readout. She tried it again, and this time when she came back, she'd realized the tests were correct. It was my worn-out blood that was faulty.

"Okay. Listen. Your iron levels are dangerously low. You have to go to the hospital right now."

I'm sure I looked like she'd smacked me in the face, because she kept going: "I'm not sure how you're functioning right now. Don't even go home to pack a bag. Just go there."

I had awoken that morning thinking it was just another day.

Despite my physician's warnings, I went home to get a few things. I felt my chances of survival would be much improved if I had a stack of books and an iPod.

I called Seth at work on the way to the hospital. He was shocked, unable to understand exactly what was happening from my imprecise rattlings, but he said he'd come to see me later on.

At the hospital, more tests were done and more questions asked of me. Seth arrived while I waited for a room. We joked around while I tried to feel hints of this sickness I had. I called my parents, told them not to worry. Called out sick from work. Late at night, I was admitted to a peach-colored room in "Jane Brown," the oldest and creepiest building in the hospital complex, an ominous 1922 mansion originally built for private (read: rich) patients, and now outmoded, dwarfed by steely, modern buildings.

In the morning, I learned that the amount of hemoglobin—the protein that transports oxygen—in my blood was at levels insufficient to keep me upright. One nurse confided, "I can't believe you haven't passed out cold by now. I've worked on oncology wards, and people with late-stage cancer have more hemoglobin than you do."

I felt like all of this was going on without me. I swore to the doctors that I felt fine, my periods were normal, I wasn't bleeding from a secret location that I wasn't telling them about. I felt tired, had skin problems, got hobbled by frequent leg cramps, and had ten years' worth of toilet issues that were once diagnosed as IBS, but I felt fine.

I was not allowed to stand up. It was that bad, I

guess, though I reminded my fave nurse that I'd not only stood, but worked all day, swam, and rode my bike a couple of days ago. "Well, now you have to lie down, and that's that," she said, tough-love style.

The next morning, an aide wheeled me, flat on a gurney, into a new part of the hospital. I received a transvaginal ultrasound; the female technician kindly showing me the skinny white wand, with its perky little spelunking light, before starting the test, the results of which showed no problems. They tested me for a bunch of rare blood diseases. All negative. I was allowed to get up to go to the bathroom for the purpose of stool sampling, but what I provided could not correctly be called a stool because that would imply it had the properties of a solid.

Guys, I've had diarrhea for ten years straight. Perhaps the problem lies there.

The doctor on my case was not my friend. He acted jolly and told me they'd figure me out, but my initial level of trust devolved quickly, and I grew to dread his visits. Like the male doctor who'd diagnosed me with IBS, he looked at me sideways, like he'd never seen a woman before and had little real desire to figure out how they worked inside. All he could do was provide a short-term dose of what my blood was lacking and send me on my way to a primary care doc, who would work out a proper diagnosis.

That day, I had a blood transfusion, just to bump me out of the dead zone. I lay in my bed watching the blood drip from the bag into my IV, half-fascinated, half-disgusted. Seth and I joked about how I'd suddenly get ripped, bulging with power, now that I had "that new blood."

The next day, they let me out. Since I'd had little to eat other than underripe honeydew melon and oversweetened yogurt during my stay, I made Seth stop immediately at a pizza place so I could load up. It was late July. It had been a gorgeous lazy summer in Providence. I wanted to go to the beach. My birthday was the next week, so we went to Martha's Vineyard. We didn't take it easy—we brought our bikes and rode them all over the island. I was still exhausted, but the short-term effect of new blood in my body, plus some B12 injections, plus the joy of not being in a hospital, buoyed me.

I had several appointments with a new primary care doc, who sent me to a gynecologist and a gastroenterologist. I was thankful for my job, which didn't pay much but came with very good health insurance. Now that the medical establishment had convinced me I really was sick, rather than just run down or getting old, I applied my usual level of doggedness to discovering the real source of my illness rather than denying its existence.

Burn Plan

During the winter at PennHenge, there is a slow-down, a time of solitude, extra sleep, and deliberate investiture in soups. The yard and the driveway fill with snow, which is then compacted into dirty ice. Leaving the house means succumbing to a list of cruel realities. While the snow falls and the wind blows, I watch, steeling myself for the inevitable shoveling escapade. After arranging my layers—socks, two pairs; giant moon boots; long underwear; jeans; sweater; scarf; ski hat; parka; down mittens—I go out to face the drifty bluster. I'm both lonely and exhilarated. Penn Street is quiet, barren, softened; there is a pleasure to the rhythm of the task at hand, and a problem-solving element to this clearing of snow from one place and piling it in another. As it goes on, though, a sharp irritation begins to slice through my meditative spell. Through the wall of the house I can hear the sounds of a first-floor tenant's video game—repetitive booms like cannon blasts. My thoughts make a hairpin turn: suddenly I'm wound up and wondering why not a single one of these dudes has even asked if I need some help. The thought of them, cozy, playing pointless video games with no concern for the world outside—a world that includes their landlady shoveling snow for an hour straight—produces enough ire to fuel me through the end of the job. Shoveling faster, I begin to mutter to myself, while now passive-aggressively heaving chunks of snow at the house, on the other side of the wall from where these guys are relaxing.

Once I'm back in soft pants and kicking it with a hot chocolate, such rage seems silly. They're renters. Snow shoveling is part of what they pay me for. It's not their problem that instead of buying a snowblower or paying the neighborhood kids to do the job, I choose to go out there and strain my own back. But there's some little bit of me that insists it would be the nice thing to do for my tenants—all men—to offer to help with this manual labor. A few minutes of their time could save an hour of mine—not because I'm a woman, but because it takes one person a lot longer to do a job than, say, three people.

But how will they know I want help if I refuse to ask for it?

They won't. And I can't.

This is one of the many subtle discomforts that arise between me and my tenants—gray areas that are complicated by the fact that I am a woman.

As a landlady, I aim to present myself as gender-neutral as possible. I'm not talking specifically about my appearance, although I only wear makeup to weddings and I'm most comfortable in hole-ridden clothes that many women would throw in the trash. I'm referring to my style of managing the house and the people within it. It seems crucial to be straightforward, to tamp down any drama; perhaps that runs counter to perceptions of how my gender handles interpersonal tasks in general. I focus on simplicity, speed, and sociability. Simplicity: I get shit done in as few steps as possible, resisting the temptation to cheap out or hold out. Speed: If the toilet breaks today, my tenants know damn well that the toilet will be fixed today. Sociability: I want to be a friend to my tenants, responsive to their concerns, not just the name on the rent check.

The place where I've failed to maintain this plan is easily identified: knee-jerk tolerance. I wanted so badly to be known as the chill landlady that I made her a close relative of the long-suffering girlfriend, readily accepting a variety of slights. Extremly late rent—as in, into-next-month late? Broken glass, messes large and small, new roommates brought in with no heads-up? "That's fine, yeah, okay," I hear myself say.

Being a woman and a feminist, and inhabiting the somewhat unusual role of landlady, I imagine that I always need to be capable and get things done without anyone's assistance. I haven't quite conceded that it's possible to take responsibility for something—even a big thing like a house—without also agreeing to do every task involved.

I also tone down the lady vibe out of self-preservation: Despite my no-nonsense way of shutting down unwanted sexual advances, I've experienced a few of them from past male tenants. They came in the form of the seemingly innocent comment ("Is it weird to tell your landlady she's pretty?"); the skeevy observation ("That is definitely a porn plot, the landlady and tenant thing?"); and the less blatant but still belittling use of terms of endearment (tenants calling me "honey" and "babe"). These quips were mostly opportunistic, casually relayed. In fact, I felt like an onlooker to these comments; they were lobbed in my general direction rather than coming confrontationally, head-on. Even if it was a novelty floating in these guys' minds, an idle sexual whim, directionless and fleeting, their voicing of it put me on alert. I have laughed at a tenant's flirtations once or twice, waving them away because doing so seemed like the fastest way to remove my body from the scene and deadbolt it in my apartment. What a luxury it must be to vocalize whatever floats along.

After several years of feeling ignored and steamrolled, though, the chill landlady had to cede control in order to preserve my mental state. Where once I would have texted, **When you have a minute, I'd really appreciate it if you'd move some of the stuff outside your apartment,** I started to say, **Front hallway is not a good storage location, please find another place for your stuff. Thanks.** That's still a few shades politer than what I want to say, which is something like, **Hey bonehead! Your bundles of cables and old canvases and random pieces of wood constitute a fire hazard and I'm sure as hell not going to let you be the reason why I can't get out of the house in a fire. REMOVE IT IMMEDIATELY.** I know how to be nice; I am learning also how to be firm and direct. I used to be so nice, and so afraid to be seen as anything but, as to squelch all meaning from my words; so many disclaimers make for an easily-ignored request. When I speak from a place of power, things get done, and Penn-Henge becomes better, safer, more peaceful. Land-ladyhood is a great training ground for doing that same thing out in the world, where it's riskier and susceptible to an endless list of veiled challenges.

That fire hazard business, by the way, is not a hypothetical; it's not something I say to my tenants just to get them to cooperate. By my count, I've witnessed six house fires on the blocks directly adjacent to mine. Usually they erupt in the very early morning; usually they are detected by my subconscious in deep sleep—silent, shocking. Some of the houses were empty; some were filled with sleeping people. No one was badly injured in any of these fires, but the experience of having just escaped your burning home must flip an internal switch that can't be deactivated. One fire happened on a top-three coldest night of the year; Seth and I quickly layered up and went outside to offer clothing to the stunned tenants in their sweatpants and T-shirts, their bodies still warm from bed and adrenaline as they expelled vaporous, swirling breath clouds. The flames shot through the roof, stretching into the sky, as we stood with them, watching the firefighters' counterattack. There wasn't much to say.

It seemed the neighborhood had surreptitiously signed up on an installment plan to burn itself down, and my mind was infected by it. The fires were drawing closer, circling around PennHenge. In daylight hours, I knew it was silly to assume the flames were coming for us, but in sleep, my brainwaves uncontrolled, I was haunted. I frequently woke up smelling phantom smoke, my teeth ground together, my tongue lumpy and numb from being bitten. To soothe myself, I checked the smoke alarms; I installed more. I begged my tenants not to smoke in the house. I ran to the window to scan the block at any unexplained sound or siren.

A friend who is a heavy dabbler in real estate once said to me, "Landlords burn down these dime-a-dozen triple deckers all the time." I was so insulted by his intimation that my house—the site of so much of my time and money—was one of many, a faceless blob not worth his notice, that I didn't parse the rest of the thought. *Landlords burn these buildings down.* It's a well-known tactic for collecting insurance money and displacing tenants from rent-subsidized apartments. (Rhode Island doesn't have a rent control program—though it should—but the state's Section 8 program offers housing vouchers and subsidies to landlords in order to create pseudo-affordable housing for low-income families.) This is literally eviction by fire. I've heard about it, I know it happens. It's still shocking to live in the center of a scorching epidemic of it.

The probability of an *accidental* fire is not all that much greater in the Hill than out in the suburbs—otherwise average suburbanites are often on the news here in Rhode Island for using a grill in the house or a blowtorch to melt ice off the gutters. Many miles of outdated wiring are to be found in the area's aging houses. There are risks, but not to the tune of six houses on three blocks. That'd be some serious bad luck. I have little choice but to believe that some of these fires are intentionally set, whether by someone with a beef against a resident or landlord, by the landlord himself, or by someone paid by the landlord. For those of us living nearby—whose homes are safe for the moment—that is both horrifying and comforting. Horrifying because it is unthinkable that any building owner would commit the disastrous act of burning down his own perfectly fine house, installing a threat to his tenants' and neighbors' safety where there would otherwise be none. Comforting because this is an intentional effort and not a fluke of wayward electricity or carelessness, and therefore, by some logic it's less likely to visit my own home. Maybe I'm a big softy, with my silly liking and appreciating of old houses, but arson just rankles me. The arsonist landlord can go back to his respectable neighborhood, his burned-out building firmly out of sight across town or across the state. He doesn't have to look at its blackened shell, but my neighbors and I do. There's the obvious possibility of hurting or killing people, endangering first responders, burning down adjacent buildings, legal consequences—starting something that can't be taken back. The idea that the law and the police and the insurance companies collectively look the other way while this goes on is just impossible for me to fathom.

There is another deduction to be made from this: that the neighborhood could be seen as beaten down to the point that no one would raise an eyebrow at this cyclical reign of destruction, where it wouldn't be a foregone conclusion that we, the people who live here, deserve better than to watch our surroundings be ravaged on the regular. As if the neighborhood is not worthy of basic subsistence, its people not worth a modicum of safety or tranquility.

Greed is a horror. Success cannot be gotten through devastation.

Whomever or whatever is responsible for these fires, the boarded-up carnage sits, and sags, and sits, often for years, as insurance checks are cashed and plans for repairs are made, or not. Some houses are eventually torn down and the wreckage carted away. Others decay in the rain and humidity until their owners get it together and fix them. The houses that are repaired are not usually restored to their pre-torched state, but fortified to a semi-acceptable level with lesser materials. (After fire damaged his large apartment building, one landlord put smaller windows well inside of the old, larger frames, literally closing in his tenants' view. It became a tidy parable for me, an image that represented the exact opposite of how I wanted to treat my tenants.)

The owner of the house right behind mine—a featureless brown three-family that Seth and I watched burn in the early hours of a spring morning—got his insurance dough and began to repair the place completely by himself, "trying to save money," he shouted down from atop his belching cherry-picker; after putting in some new windows and beginning to work on the roof and siding, he stopped appearing. The tarps on the roof became ripped and frayed, slapping in on themselves as years of harsh weather slowly destroyed them. Wind and rain permeated the walls, where I'd bet a large pile of insurance money that ponderous amounts of mold formed. A family of birds took up messy residence in the open roof; industrious mice shimmied through holes at ground level. The yard filled with weeds and out-of-control vegetable plants. Eventually, someone came around and clear-cut it all, but they didn't even bother to go inside the house.

Because I may never get my first choice—to see this house restored to some kind of working order—I take my consolation prize: I watch it try to return to the earth. It's a fun study to undertake, as long as I stuff down my human need to see things used in accordance with their potential and purpose.

It doesn't take long before you stop seeing the damage and the modern ruins and board-ups become a rote part of the neighborhood. Old ruins are sexy, prized, visited, appreciated. New ruins? They only symbolize failure. If you live amid new ruins, you have to constantly remember not to take them as an indicator of your own worth in the world.

My guts were still feeling like the flesh-and-blood equivalent of that damaged house, but my new primary care doc was hopeful. She was all business, brisk but friendly, and she was dead serious about cracking my case. After my summertime hospital stay, I spent the fall shuttling to specialist after specialist, relaying the latest developments and getting accustomed to watching doctors' eyes widen when they saw the results of my hospital bloodwork.

Then I saw a gastroenterologist. She was young; she was driven; she was upbeat. I had a feeling I was nearing the end of this crisis of not knowing. I visualized taking a normal poop, and it seemed like a beautiful, otherworldly dream.

She scheduled me for a colonoscopy, an endoscopy, and a variety of blood tests.

I prepped for the colonoscopy with dire faith, drinking the criminally disgusting colon bleach provided until I barfed it back out.

Seth brought me in, waited during the procedure, and kindly listened to my daffy anesthesia-induced digressions afterward.

The next day, my gastroenterologist called.

"Okay, so I have some news. You have celiac disease. The blood test detected the antibodies, and we confirmed the diagnosis with the endoscopy. It's severe in that you have a lot of internal damage to your small intestine. It's kind of an off-the-charts case."

"Uhhh, okay!" I said excitedly. I didn't yet want to think about what this meant, but I had a feeling this was the diagnosis I should have gotten years ago, and I didn't want her to think I couldn't handle it.

"So, this means you are going to have to cut out gluten from your diet. Wheat, barley, and rye are making you very sick. You have to get down to a molecular level, like, check your toothpaste, things like that."

"Umm . . ."

"But that's the best part—the treatment isn't a drug, it's just a dietary change!" she went on.

"Mmhmm."

"You can do it! It's going to be hard for a little while, but I bet you'll feel a lot better the next time you see me."

"Okay. Thank you. Yeah, I can do it, I'll figure it out," I said.

"You're welcome! Good luck! Let us know how you're doing!"

I staggered around my kitchen in a daze, trashing anything and everything that had gluten in it, googling anything with vague labeling. I held a canister of flour, turned it in my hands, and watched the grains slide against each other, before dumping it.

I was too tired to give much thought to what I *could* eat, so for a week I consumed mostly corn tortilla chips and salsa.

Crunching, I thought bitterly of all the things I would NEVER EAT AGAIN—EVER: burritos, pizza, beer, pasta, donuts, bagels, pie. A simple freaking roll or a fresh, chewy slice of bread. A damn brioche! I would never get to try a single croque monsieur, whether I wanted to or not. A friend of mine with a severe gluten allergy relayed that for a while after she went gluten-free, she desired to punch any person she saw eating a tasty-looking piece of bread. Emotionally, I went the other way: I cried and had to leave the room when I found myself the only gluten abstainer in a group of friends luxuriating in really good pizza.

The strangest part was that I'd never again be able to pick something up and eat it without considering its every ingredient.

Before I could dissolve into self-pity, though, Seth started cooking for me. He took no shortcuts. He did not fall for inadequate wheat analogs like gluten-free bread or fake pasta. Instead he bought the best, simplest ingredients he could find, and took a lot of care to prepare them in healing ways. He was never annoyed with my new restriction; he took it as a chance to learn. The damage to my body couldn't be undone in a week, a month, or even a year, but his understated care bolstered me, helped me start to mend.

I occasionally saw Neil around town for six months or so after his disgraced flight from PennHenge. I fumed at him from across several rooms. He worked as a bartender at one of my standard spots for a while, and wordlessly pushed free drinks at me. Then he quickly vanished from town, seemingly no more than a damaging apparition.

The second-floor apartment again went empty for a few months while I cleaned it, mellowed the residue of rage, and hired a "friend price" contractor acquaintance to make it suitable for mentally stable people to live in: new refrigerator, new stove, antique tub installed, new toilet, new drywall in the bathroom, antique light fixtures, and farmhouse sink in the kitchen. Even as I shifted my paltry money around and leaned heavily on my credit cards, I scraped the bottom of my checking account every other week to pay him. The apartment was still spare and bare, but I was proud to have improved it to the point at which nothing was broken or close to it. Now it was only in desperate need of humans who cared, even a little.

I had to make sure the apartment didn't fall into the wrong hands yet again. I was reluctant—almost afraid—to count on myself to accomplish this task. I had again and again gladly palmed the keys over to people who immediately began to take extreme liberties. I used to be a strong judge of character, but I could no longer claim that knack. Best to rely on a known quantity; best to rely on someone I had found trustworthy before my powers of discernment had left me. I really needed a friend, a *good friend,* to move in.

My old buddy Dan and his husband-to-be Steve were moving to Rhode Island after a stint in Phoenix, and I decided they'd be my saviors. I would not accept them moving anywhere but to PennHenge. Dan is one of my favorite human beings on the planet; he was and is one of the most original, creative, and tenaciously loyal people I've ever known. James and I had lived with him in Boston for a couple of years, and the three of us had gotten close. Dan taught me how to cook; I brought him to the hospital when he broke his collarbone. We perfected our own brand of a droll nihilist communication style. He had his quirks—loudly coming home at 4:00 a.m., drunkenly singing along to Xiu Xiu; taking baths so long my roommates and I had to knock and make sure he was still alive; providing lengthy descriptions of his new-favorite-record-of-the-week, which tracks were best, and why. Ever politically incorrect, his standard joke was to ask me where I'd been and—

regardless of my answer—suggest that I'd actually been turning tricks in the nearest subway station. There was another one about how he'd come home to find me crumpled in the bushes, with my hair a mess and "one pump on." For every crack lovingly chucked in my direction, he doubly made fun of James, lampooning him for his overbitter worldview.

Dan is my brother. I love the man very much.

Steve and I got along great the few times we'd hung out. And I liked these two together. They had three dogs—two Boston terriers and a Chihuahua— who were all deranged and hilarious. I visualized a happily chaotic scene, lots of booze and grilling, game nights, goofing off, the dogs weaving paths among us. I presented this cozy picture to Dan and Steve, and they decided to take the place—or possibly, I pushed until they relented.

I still had the summer months to kill before the boys could leave Phoenix and attempt a cross-country move, and another friend, Dennis, needed a place to stay in the meantime. Dennis is an honorable, funny, big, bearded guy who is extraordinarily beloved around town—the sort of guy who'd sacrifice just about anything for you if he loves you while simultaneously having little use for the bulk of society, for the law, for religion, for a job, for money. As a touring musician, he kept his financial obligations at a minimum and relied on fast food, chance, and the kindness of friends. Safeguarding my sanity as I was, and looking for a good person rather than a moneyed person, I told him he could stay in the second-floor place for the summer; it was no problem. (I had gone back to taking on freelance editing work so that I could pay the extra chunk of the mortgage while the place was empty.) Dennis agreed to help me with a few projects around the house and slide me a "hundo" when he had it.

Dennis moved in—though it could hardly be called moving when one's possessions consist of a tiny TV set, an Xbox, a milk crate stuffed with black T-shirts, a sleeping bag, a bike, and a wetsuit. Oh, and a couple of firearms, which I allowed him for some senseless reason to store (sans ammo, at least) in the basement. Dennis spent a good part of the summer at PennHenge, being my buddy and helping me paint and fix things occasionally. He slept directly on the floor—no mattress, no pillow, just a beat-up sleeping bag—and had a snore for the ages. Somehow, I found his snore comforting. Subjectively, I could overlook this momentous chest rattle, which could be heard from almost anywhere in the house, and probably next door, because I liked the rattler himself; coming from someone like Dougie Peppers, the same sound would have been grounds for eviction.

As was now our Fourth of July tradition, Seth and I had another true-to-form power holiday—biking to his parents' place for the now-requisite parade viewing, grilling session, badminton, and bay kayaking. He moved with alarming speed between leisure activities, and again I struggled to keep up without copping to my exhaustion. In the afternoon we returned to Providence, noted with bemusement that the neighborhood had not lost any of its gusto for fireworks, and escaped again on our bikes. Winding our way through the West End streets, we chose one that was unofficially closed to traffic because of a large family barbecue. Seeing a pair of uninvited guests show up, a swarm of kids on bikes quickly tightened around us, yelling at us to get off their street and half-assedly trying to knock us off our bikes. As we turned onto the next block unscathed, we howled with laughter, caught our breath, and continued on.

Our destination was a house show in a desolate area of Providence dominated by a decaying highway, where a bunch of bands were playing in a garage. This was a cheery crowd of not-very-nationalistic musicians and artists; we fed off of the general din, the copious beer (cider for me), the block party atmosphere, and each other, happily immersing ourselves in the rare feeling that we might all be okay because even in a country full of twits we had this, a community of headstrong and smart people with good beliefs and good instincts.

I gazed at Seth across the asphalt, watched him talk music with a friend. We were moving along at a comfortable clip; we were close, we understood one another. We made each other more adventurous and more lighthearted. We maintained a spirited independence—even at this party we stayed social and didn't stick to each other—but we considered one another's needs; we diverted our routines to make time. We had fun, but we got deep. We traveled together well. This person loved me; there were times I knew it. I didn't need him to say it. And I loved him too: his thoughtfulness and his confidence and his lack of pretense. We were too evolved to be cloying. It was exhilarating to love someone without requiring confirmation of his feelings for me. It was a little like being at the edge of a cliff.

People My Age

Having given Providence a last round of his legendary sweaty bear hugs, Dennis moved far from us, and I waited for Dan and Steve to make their own cross-country trek in my direction. They arrived in November. We had a jubilant reunion, hugging, jumping, yelping, being leapt upon by their dogs. But we all felt new stresses closing in almost immediately. Their moving truck was weeks late, and some of their stuff was broken on arrival. Dan quickly became depressed when he couldn't find a job in deep-recession Providence; at the time of their move, Rhode Island had the highest unemployment rate in the country.

With Steve at work all day, Dan spent the mornings applying for jobs, and the afternoons taking solitary walks around the wintry city, picking up industrial garbage or cast-off building materials and stuffing them into his backpack. When I'd arrive home from work, I found he'd employed the materials in decorating, first his own apartment, and then the back stairwell. After a couple of weeks of his immersion in this task, patinaed bricks, thick bolts, bits of old rope, rusty film reels, and dried flower wreaths mingled with small bits of artwork all the way up to my apartment door. It looked great—a juxtaposition of harsh and soft—but I worried that Dan wasn't happy in the house, or in Providence, and that his busy beautification was born out of serious anxiety.

The boys and I had a great time together, making dinners and listening to music, but it was clear that something was bothering them. The first-floor dudes partied loudly and stayed up late, doing little to curtail the noise even when Steve went downstairs to plead for quiet. And they felt bad about their dogs, who barked and tore up the grass in the yard. I knew pretty quickly that living at PennHenge wasn't suited to them, but I hoped that when Dan found a job and life cooled into a routine, our arrangement might be more appealing.

A few months in, though, Steve came upstairs to officially let me know they'd be breaking their lease and moving to a new place, a freestanding house with a huge fenced yard for the dogs. He was appropriately contrite about it, but I felt ditched, as if they were saying the house wasn't good enough for them. "Okay, so because we're friends, I have to let you break the lease? And I have no recourse? Seems like a shitty thing to do to a friend. Yeah, leave. Do whatever you want." Steve's face fell, and he quietly apologized and hurriedly retreated.

I couldn't have expected them to stay, especially after those first few telling weeks. I had dragged them into living at PennHenge half-knowing it wasn't really what they were looking for, so why was I surprised to have them confirm it for me? I was irritated by my fragility. When would I stop receiving this news defensively, like I was being broken up with?

Not one to let an argument fester, I apologized to Steve and Dan the next day; in fact, it was more of an apology fest, as I apologized to Steve and Dan and each of them apologized to me and to each other. I owned up to feeling rejected and to irrational thoughts about the house's inferiority, and we had a big GF dinner and laughed it off. Our love for each other fully restored, they agreed to do a few extra things in exchange for being able to break their lease. Dan offered to list the apartment on Craigslist and to bravely field the incoming phone calls. Still not ready to get back on the horse after the gravity of the Neil experience, I gratefully agreed.

Dan had good instincts. He meticulously screened out Craigslist crazies and set me up to show the place to a guy named Eric, who would be moving in with his girlfriend Jess. They'd been living in a cramped and loud little apartment right here in Federal Hill; the landlord was a dick and they were ready to get out.

Eric was so thin he looked brittle; though he was twenty-five, he could have passed for a high school kid. He wore glasses and sported a Pearl Jam stick-figure-boy logo tattoo on his ankle. While the latter feature would normally be the first, second, and third strikes against him, I forced myself to stay impartial and judge this guy on his personality and smarts, rather than on superficial features, which had only gotten me in trouble in the past. He was an affable guy, a little jumpy. He had a tendency to ramble, but in a way I could hang with. He was also gainfully employed, responsible, and (over email) asked a multitude of bright questions in full sentences *and* with punctuation. Was I actually going to live with a Pearl Jam fan club member? It was looking that way.

The next time we met, Eric brought Jess. She, like he, was from a little town in upstate New York, a smart, curious, and friendly lady with a nervous air and a rather amazing head of fluffy, curly black hair. She worked from home, so she'd be around most of the time, keeping an eye on the place. She had no immediately visible Pearl Jam tattoos.

They were in.

Their arrival heralded a shift in the age dynamics of my landladyhood. Eric and Jess may have been the first tenants whom I thought of as "young" and not just "around my age." It's an odd prism through which I've watched myself get older. So I've observed Eric—who is still here at PennHenge today, bless him—as he navigated his mid- to late twenties, and hit thirty. He and Jess split up after a year or so of living together here; she was his tether to their more conservative hometown and his teenage self. When she left, he became free to break out and see who he was. He's a goofball and a good person. He's had a few whacked-out girlfriends and roommates; he's been beaten up on the street; he's flown around the world to see Pearl Jam (still don't get that one); he's developed into something of a beer and bong aficionado. He's become a formidable long-distance runner. He handloo crises the way I do: calmly, with bemusement, without overreaction. He rarely complains, and although he constantly forgets his keys, he is otherwise reliable and steadfast. All of this is great for stability, because his roommates have been so numerous that I can't remember all of their names.

Eric has become a specialist in the area of sublets and short-stay roommates. I'm not sure whether he just loves having a variety of freewheeling people around or whether he is secretly fleecing them for extra rent, or both, but during the summer months the extra room turns over monthly. Sometimes the additional human in question is Eric's good friend; sometimes she/he is a minor acquaintance. One of his friends crashed with us for six months while he was going through a complicated breakup that involved a co-owned house. One of my favorite short-termers, with us at the same time, was a rakish surfer guy named Kerry who seemed completely comfortable wherever he found himself—like the universe was at his confident command but he was choosing to keep it casual and not exploit his power. He's exceedingly smart and had some visionary freelance tech job that I couldn't iterate if you paid me. He traveled to far-flung locales for activist and artistic causes. He blasted electronic dance music; he was mostly naked most of the time. He and his gorgeous girlfriend had loud sex that made my entire apartment shake mightily. His motto was "No stress, man," which coming from him was somehow inspiring and not at all vapid.

Because Eric works for an arts organization that

sponsors learning and tech incubator programs of various lengths, he's always meeting international geniuses who need a friendly place to stay for a few weeks. There was a web developer from Brazil, a cute Peruvian digital experimentalist and occasional DJ, and an Indian physicist and mathematician. To my horror, Eric also invited an eighteen-year-old girl from Wisconsin to stay for a good chunk of one summer. I had visions of this young person, away from her family at last, slamming down shots and dancing on tables somewhere. I implored Eric to *watch this girl, do not leave her unattended for long.* I told him I'd need to meet her as soon as she arrived so I could get all Mom on her and explain the rules.

I sat her down at the picnic table and looked her over. She was rather adorable: short hair, glasses, a T-shirt with a comic book character on it, jeans, an artist's manner. She had a diminutive but determined voice. But I couldn't let her innocent appearance sway me from the intelligence I was collecting. I told her that, in a way, I was substituting for her parents while she was staying at PennHenge, and that even though she was on her own for a little while, she could always call me or Eric if she needed anything. No drinking, no drugs. She was unmoved by my speech. A little haughtily, she said, "Ugh. I hope I never even want to *try* drinking. It's *so* disgusting." The more we talked, she voiced further repulsion with the way most people her age behaved and the things they liked and found important, a stance I would have echoed in nearly the same words at age eighteen. Compared to this young woman, though, at that age I was Sid Vicious. I'd imagined a need to shield her from all the pitfalls of city living as a young adult, but she turned it around on me. As the summer went on, she openly judged the PennHenge crowd for every "bad" behavior we exhibited—really just wine and cigarettes, staying up late, and being loud—and she and I talked it through. It was rather bold of her to speak up, and I was cool with her criticisms because I'm twice her age and I have a soft spot for complicated young people.

I never registered the fact that I was only a year older than her when I got my first apartment, and that the landlady, sweet Mrs. Caruso, never sat me or my roommates down to tell us what not to do. She certainly never claimed to be a parental proxy.

I had pictured this young woman alone in a new city, with a bunch of comparatively old weirdos around, and wondered if she would know what to do. She did.

Right before she left, she told me she planned to change her name when she returned to Wisconsin. She had picked out a futuristic name that sounded like an anime character. She was really going to do it; she was excited to shrug off her parents and her high school friends and make this bold move. It made me remember the delicate nature of eighteen, how hard it can be to have no idea who you'll turn out to be, while being perfectly aware of that fact. She was putting her bet on the table with this new name—wagering that it would help her become tough and spirited and arty, and not spend time fretting about what "people her age" did.

Months after she left, Eric told me that our young friend was trans. Her summer in Providence was her first real time away from home as a woman. Apparently, she knew more about who she'd turn out to be than I'd given her credit for.

Rumblings

Over the years, the goals for my apartment have gone from radical—a rooftop geodesic dome and garden were once considered—to ordinary. Basic maintenance has become enough for me. I thought by now this place would be under tight control, clean, of a piece, thoughtfully arranged. But just buying a house did not turn me into an orderly person. In a sense, the house and I are a perfect match: we're both willing to accept a little defeat, even as we go on trying to self-improve.

I'm a fully formed, set-in-my-ways old lady now, just like the house, and we both have to make peace with one unpleasant fact about me: I am no domestician. I have avoided admitting this personal flaw since I slouched into my first apartment, hoping it might not be a permanent part of my personality. I'm not a total slob, but I am indifferent to spotlessness. When I clean something, I irrationally expect it to stay clean indefinitely. If I scrubbed the bathroom sink two weeks ago, I'll feel that a grave injustice has occurred upon noticing that a layer of toothpaste spittle has formed.

That I don't delight in keeping my apartment white-glove ready is not so awful. But couple that trait with my poor understanding of spatial organization and tendency toward inertia in all things decorating, and the result is a failing score on the Marie Kondo scale. It's not that I have an emotional urge to hold on to things—I actually relish trashing stuff I no longer use—it's that once I put something somewhere, I stop seeing it. I just start working around it. Because my apartment has only one closet, a lot of things just have to be left out in the open. Piles of things—books, mostly—seem unlikely ever to move again. And if I start a project that goes unfinished, the cans of paint or jugs o' spackle might sit for months before being relegated to the basement, because *I was just about to get to that.*

My internal shakiness is echoed by the house in a very real way. While I'm perched in my third-floor hideaway, with no warning, the flowerpots and the canisters of rice and tea rattle against each other. A subtle clanking is heard. The walls waver, delicately but unmistakably. The couch or the bed trembles for a minute, stops, trembles again.

The first time I felt this, I was absolutely certain that it was a mild earthquake. I ran to my computer to check Facebook and the local news. No corroboration. I looked outside. No commotion; no one streaming into the street. Nothing at all out of the ordinary. So, then, I had to accept that the shaking was limited to my own house. Must've been a fluke, I thought: *A crew is working on something underground down the street, and it's vibrating houses blocks away.*

But it didn't stop. The next time it happened, I froze, panicked, suddenly wondering what it would look like to be in this room when the house collapsed. How exactly would the physics of such a thing order themselves? What would move first? Would I know what was happening before I fell through the floor? How many seconds would it take? What would it sound like? My previous stress dream of chewing my own teeth was replaced by an exotic new offering in which the floors cracked horrendously, and, still encased in my bed, I tumbled through a menacing hole straight into molten earth, followed by enormous chunks of the walls and a selection of my earthly effects.

Eventually that shaky feeling lodged itself in my brain and made me worry about the structural viability of the house. In hopes of fixing the problem, I sought out a contractor to take on the undesirable job of repairing the foundation of the house.

The first guy who came to take a look said he had some ideas, but thought it best to "wait until your husband gets home" to discuss them in detail. Wouldn't want to stress the delicate little wifey by talking dollars and cents, I guess. I croaked, "You're going to be waiting a *long* time," and dismissed him.

The second guy didn't speculate on my marital status, but his proposal was to cover the deteriorating bricks with a skim coat of mortar, and then a sealant. Considering there was little more than dust for the mortar to hold on to, this seemed a bit too simplistic to really fix the problem.

The third guy, Nathaniel, was smart and fearless, an old-school New Englander with a square body and a funny, good-naturedly crass attitude.

He was just what I needed: a wiseass who couldn't have cared less about my personal particulars. He was the house's savior at that moment, an old house whisperer who unquestioningly understood my efforts to keep the house largely as it was. I hired him, and the poor guy spent the best days of the summer in the damp, dusty underground of PennHenge, excising brick after rotted brick until there was something solid to build on, restoring sections of walls, and even shoring up one part, cracked top to bottom, with another cinder block interior wall "just to be safe." He rebuilt parts of the chimney, jacking it up temporarily and risking serious hurt to replace the pulverized bricks at the bottom. Nathaniel did a fantastic, even heroic job, in exchange for $9,000, a.k.a., the very bottom of my recently rebuilt savings account, plus further payments to him as my paychecks straggled through. The bill was scary, but I figured any job that lasts an entire summer and carries a very real risk of being crushed by a chimney should pay at least that much.

Alas, the shaking continued unabated. I'd spent some very real money to fix a phantom problem. Hell, the basement certainly *looked* better, and pieces no longer came off in my hands at the slightest provocation, so all was not lost. When he came back to collect a payment, I asked Nathaniel what might be going on, and he wisely counseled me, "It's probably just that one of the couples downstairs is *on a schedule*. You get me?"

I spent $9,000 to counter the motion in someone's ocean. And I lost.

Safety. So much of what we do is a search for it. The structures we build—physical and emotional—are aimed at keeping us warm and dry and ignorant of the fact that others are having sex directly below us.

By now, Johnny the body piercer had left the first floor due to financial troubles; he'd been replaced in brief turns by a couple of Elvin's girlfriends (one at a time) and then a sulky red-haired couple with a dopey red-haired dog. When they left, Elvin's best friend Kenny moved in, and these two have lived in harmonious platonic manly bliss ever since.

I love Kenny. Everyone loves Kenny. He's charming, he's loyal, he's a joker, he knows how to have a conversation. People like being around him. However, Kenny is a big man with big hands that seem to inadvertently crush everything they touch. He's a bartender and restaurant manager and never comes home before 3:00 a.m.; after a few beers, usually very late at night, he can rip a doorknob clear off or break a window without even noticing it, leaving the damage behind until I happen upon it the next morning and confusedly clean it up. He once parked his Toyota behind my car, and proceeded to leave its headlights on and go to bed—in the morning he had a dead battery but was so deeply asleep that he couldn't be roused to help push his dead car out to the street. Another time he broke the glass in the house's main entry door; in the morning, as I swept up the jagged bits, I seized upon a stinky container of takeout food with Kenny's name written on it, a full can of beer right next to it, as if he were preemptively claiming responsibility and stating the cause of his mistake.

These two may be happy living together, but over their years of cohabitating, they've forgotten what it means to clean things, to maintain their living space in even the simplest of ways.

I learned just how far it had gone when there was a plumbing emergency in their apartment. Kenny took a predawn shower, then discovered he couldn't turn off the water. He went to the basement and started turning off valves to try to cut off the water flow to his bathroom. When that didn't stop the deluge, my phone dinged with his text. I only flipped over and hugged my pillow. Upon the second ding, I started to drift slightly out of sleep. After a few minutes of groggily willing myself to stumble the six feet over to my phone's charging perch, I managed to put my feet on the floor. The text read, **Sorry to get you so late, the shower won't stop running, I tried shutting off all the valves in the basement but to no avail.** Learning of the problem in a nearly somnambulant state, my yearning to go back to bed overtaking all worldly considerations, I texted back: **That's a weird one. Nothing we can do about it now. I'll call plumber in a few hours.**

I flopped back into bed and stubbornly closed my eyes. A minute later, they popped open again as I gained enough consciousness to figure out that this problem was not to be slept through. I shut off the main water intake to the house—by then my classic fix-all for any plumbing issue—and *then* went back to sleep.

A few hours later, the plumber arrived. His face, not exactly a picture of workplace enthusiasm, only sagged further when he saw Elvin and Kenny's apartment. This was the furthest I'd ventured into the apartment in half a decade, and it was alarmingly worse than I expected. The plumber and I stood inelegantly in the tiny bathroom, the smell of caked-on urine rising from a crusty toilet; the shower seemed never to have seen a scrub. As we spoke, my eyes darted out to the kitchen, where literal piles of dank trash lay on the floor. There was a layer of dirt on every surface and a general staleness that suggested everything had been permeated by smoke, despite the many overtures I'd made about smoking outside. Blankets covered some of the windows, leaving the place dark and stifling. Show posters and pieces of art masked every wall, overlapping each other in a crowded mass. The scene reminded me of the punk squats and underground art and music venues I've visited, made and managed by a variety of dissident visionaries. But those spaces were full of energy, bursting with a thrilling, playful spirit of fun and ingenuity. This apartment was still and stagnant, as if it were decomposing a little each day.

The plumber was still talking, but my brain stem wandered off, currently engaged as it was in an inner monologue that had taken over the minute I stepped into the apartment: *Holy shit. I really haven't been on top of checking this place over, have I?*

I've avoided dropping in on these guys, but I thought I could . . . trust them? I mean, garbage piles? Is this a frat house? I have to do something. I have to ask them to leave. The place needs to be gutted, cleaned, overhauled—and rented again, but to whom? A nice couple with office jobs and sensible desires?

The monologue freezes at that point, shorts out, starts over. I extricate myself from the plumbing discussion and try to shake off the surprise of what I've just seen. I know I can't allow these guys to continue to unintentionally ruin the only thing of value that I own, the object of a decade-plus of my love and dismay. In a way, I hate them for putting me in this position, for showing so little respect. But I've let it fall into a serious rut; I've been so hands-off as to suggest I am unconcerned with getting the place up to the lowest standards.

For perspective, I check out apartment listings— NEWLY RENOVATED!—and I'm repulsed by the cheap sameness. Every kitchen has the same faux fancy tile; the same bland cabinetry. This is what the landlords of the world consider nice and modern, what they seek higher and higher rents for these days. I can't turn the ruined first-floor apartment into a clean facade with no soul, a Home Depot ad of generic splendor; I can't scrub the grime so hard that I discover there's nothing of substance here. I am no longer interested in channeling upmarket aspirations through PennHenge.

What I really want is to release all the anxiety I have stored up in the house over these years, to let it combust in a colossal fireball of the mind. To untangle all the means by which PennHenge has been a vessel for my larger fears.

On a warm spring day, inspired by the purchase of a few flats of seedlings, Seth and I built new raised garden beds to replace the ones Dean and I had put in six or so years prior, which were no longer holding together. We removed the rotted wood frames and bracketed new wood together, driving the new structures into the footprints left in the dark soil, nestling them in with hilled-up dirt. The garden was just perking up again after the hard freeze of winter, the first green nubs beginning to overtake the soil. It was a lovely day, but our conversation was unusually terse, and the task illogically grim. Our celebratory high-five was limp. I couldn't reverse his malaise with even my best-intentioned jokes or stories or affection. I felt a twinge at the periphery of my consciousness, and I promptly squeezed my eyes shut to blot it away.

But the axis had shifted, and the shift had come so fast as to stupefy me. The next morning, as we lounged in bed, Seth was quiet. I prodded him to tell me what was wrong, meanwhile assuring myself that it had nothing to do with me, when he said, "I just keep wondering if we might be better as friends."

I launched directly into a panic attack.

In six years, this was the first time he had ever voiced such a thought.

What could I do with this new information?

How could I not have seen this coming?

In that moment I was filled with new, unwelcome knowledge. I knew then that I would never have a child—although I'd never really pictured myself as a mother, the suddenness of the thought was painful. I knew in a flash that I had tricked myself, and I was filled with grief for the ill-defined union we had divined.

I was angry at him for withholding so much, and I was afraid of being without him.

Only fleetingly in the first few years did I worry about a "future." We never wanted to judge our thing by our parents' yardstick; we just wanted to have fun. We admired each other deeply; we contained the same ratio of cynical versus dreamy; our affinities matched. While I stayed silent on naming what we had, all was well. But lately I'd been trying to get him to quantify it, select words for it. Once or twice, I had obliquely hinted that he might want to move in with me—frowning, he blurted, "I don't want to live here. This is your place." I'd been tiptoeing around the big questions in our relationship, not asking for much because I feared those point-blank answers.

I had been attempting to coerce a long lifespan for us. After six years together, I started to think I could ask for that. But I discovered that even after that long, there were still many things I could not say to him.

Still, I tried to hold on. That summer was a sad exercise in groveling. I made myself as appealing as possible: I was cute, I made no demands. In the fall, after hovering in a frustrating stasis for several months, we spent a miserable couple of days in coastal Maine. Again and again, I tried to lighten the mood, and again he would frown, sigh, refuse to be touched. When we got back to town, I dropped him off at his place. I called him a few minutes later and asked, "Are we breaking up?"

"I don't know," he said, but the bleakness in his tone contained the answer.

Still, I didn't let go. I chased his affection; if I got it once or twice, I quickly assumed that the trouble had passed and we could resume a fully devoted relationship, only to reinjure myself when I learned it was only a momentary reprieve.

All this time I'd thought it was magical that he only told me he loved me in the middle of the night, when he would stir momentarily, murmur the words in my ear, and gather me up in his arms, falling away again and leaving me wide awake and unsettled. He didn't seem to remember it in the morning. Once, during my second post-breakup groveling period, I mentioned these utterings, and he turned red, chuckled, and said only, "Oh."

I only told him I loved him after we broke up. I blabbered the words through tears and spit and let the snot run down my face as I erupted with the devotion and fear I'd been afraid to acknowledge in our years together.

Sometimes I put the blame on PennHenge, for being a tether, for holding me down. If only I didn't have the house, I'd think, *then* he'd want to live with me, even marry me. I didn't allow myself to believe that these things were simply not for us to do together.

In my singlehood, the house became a welcome burden. It received my renewed attention. I found plenty of time to clean it, paint it, make my apartment a calming force, rearrange furniture as an exercise in moving on. It was my old friend; it hugged me in its warmth when I came home from a day or two away, and it silently remained where I left it, a needle poised over a record, waiting for something to play. All that winter, I abandoned my usual frugality and cranked the heat, because it got cold in the old house at night.

Settling into forced winter solitude, I spent a lot of time baldly assessing my body and my mind, and I decided that both were pretty sound, despite the circumstances. Most crucially, I had discovered what it's like not to live with illness every day. My troubles didn't exactly vanish overnight when I went gluten-free—I had a lot of healing to do, and it took so long I thought maybe my digestive system was a lost cause. But that poor, ravaged pit did rebuild itself. I felt a momentous joy upon realizing—a full three years after my celiac diagnosis—that I was not destined to a life that revolved around unpleasant toilet experiences. I would no longer be imprisoned by my own shit, at least not in a literal sense.

Celiac had caused a web of complications in my body. Daily leg and foot cramps. Skin problems. Bizarre, rapid-onset headaches that felt like a bloom in my skull. I had no idea these were connected to my larger illness until they receded completely as my digestive hassles diminished.

If you're considering a chronic autoimmune disease—they're big these days—may I recommend celiac? Aside from a longing for beer, bread, and elaborate desserts, it's been all right for me. I fixed it without drugs or protracted hospitalization. And now I know how it feels to steal my life back from that dark force. The disease had diminished me; a foggy horizon once closed in, obscuring so much of me. It almost had me, but I escaped.

Baby Grand

One morning, I heard a lot of noise downstairs—sounds of furniture being moved, stuff being dropped, dudes living in a dudely way. I shrugged it off, as I have become adept at doing. A few minutes later, though, my phone buzzed. The text message, from Eric, read, **In case you're wondering, Colin has decided to bring his piano to Penn St. Piano movers and all.**

Colin, the newest recruit in Eric's cavalcade of roommates, had just arrived in the house. We hadn't had a proper conversation yet, though I had tried. He moved in under the guise of a very short sublet, but then decided to stay. I would run into him in the hall or on the driveway, and I'd attempt to welcome him or ask a question, but halfway through the first sentence, I would falter to a stop because he appeared to be absolutely terrified of me. He stared at me, ashen, slack-jawed, eyes locked wide. He answered with a stilted word or two, and we both hurried away. Our relationship having started thusly, I was a bit unsure of his presence, but as usual I figured it would all work out fine. Then: the piano text.

This was one of those rare times when I would have to confront an interpersonal situation in progress. Exploiting my bubbling adrenaline, I took a look down the front stairwell to check out the scene. Colin stood, hands in pockets, watching four grunting gentlemen try to hoist a massive object up the narrow, winding staircase.

Blinking, clearing my throat, I said something like, "Hey, how's it goin'? What's going on here?"

Colin explained nervously that he was having his piano moved in. "It's a baby grand."

"I can see that, yeah," I said. "You gonna just . . . put it in your room here?" The open door to Colin's bedroom revealed that a baby grand-sized space had been cleared.

"Yeah, right here in my room."

"Okay, huh. Well, I wish you'd mentioned it before the fact," I said.

"Oh. I'm really sorry, yeah, I probably should have," Colin said.

At this point I unearthed a little speech that I bring out whenever someone in the house has done something implausible: "Listen, I really want you to enjoy living here. I want *all of us* to enjoy living here. That sort of means we all have to respect each other, y'know? We're in close quarters here, and we have to keep in mind how we're affecting other people."

"I'm really sorry. I'm so sorry. I should have talked to you," Colin said.

This conversation went on a little longer, as the four movers continued their brave struggle, one man getting underneath the piano and crawling up the stairs with it balanced on his back, the others guiding and lifting it as much as they could. Colin, who shares his surname with an old-money New

England family, seemed totally unfazed by this feat of manual labor, and I started to get the feeling he'd been waited on a lot in his young life. Irritated by Colin's obstinacy—he just *stood* there—I went back into my apartment and shut the door. Turned out, they couldn't get the piano all the way up the stairs after all, though they did leave a few giant gouges in the wall, requiring an additional trip for purposes of patching. I would have gladly accepted the holes in the wall not to have to listen to this guy play the piano all day and night, and then move out in a few months, at which point this hulking thing would have to be borne back *out* of the house by some further act of heroic strength.

Later, Colin came upstairs to apologize again, and we had something resembling a fruitful conversation. He told me he'd "come from a pretty unconventional living situation" (something about a big, rambling, falling-down house), and as such, he was unfamiliar with the required niceties of living at PennHenge. He mentioned that the baby grand had actually been *left outside* for the past couple of years, so it was really beat up and warped anyway, and "sounded crazy." He'd told the movers to "just throw it away." Of course, he still had to pay hundreds of dollars to the moving company, despite the fact that the object of his affection was on its way to the landfill.

In those first few months after his arrival, I cynically decided that Colin was slumming—just gathering some street cred on his way to bigger and better things. He was only twenty-two, and it was the first time he'd lived on his own. But over the summer, perhaps six months after he moved in, Colin started on a home improvement tear. Not a Neil-style episode involving sledgehammer-based destruction, but a set of positive, well-executed changes that made the place look better and feel more comfortable. First, he painted his own room. It had been a rather awful shade of flat electric blue, sloppily painted by the illustrious Neil and then left that color by several subsequent occupants. Colin could not abide. So he bought some paint in a very dignified old-hotel sort of gray, and he went for it. He didn't let me know in advance; I was coming home one night and looked up and saw that the room was suddenly a different color. I thought, if I can just impress upon this guy that someone other than him *owns* this place, and that he needs to inform that person of any changes he wants to make, we are going to work together just fine. A few weeks later, Eric offhandedly mentioned in an email that Colin was "turning his space into a fancy hotel room." I began to relish my evening walks back to the house, so I could creep around and look up to spy on the latest embellishments surreptitiously being made to my own home. One night, it was a chandelier with a multitude of tiny lampshades on it; another time, a flat-screen TV mounted on the wall. I had to admit that the place was looking pretty baller; there's nothing wrong with milk crates and lumpy Ikea sofas, but Colin's tastes and resources well exceeded that level. The next time I stopped into the apartment, he had done the kitchen as well, painting the room in multiple shades of a very modern soft purple-gray that somehow also completely fit the look of the house. He'd installed track lighting and it shone on nice pieces of framed art. For a moment I thought, *Why would anyone do all this work to a rental? He's going to extort money from me now, in payment for these interior design services.*

But actually, it's been the opposite. I made the rare move of speaking directly to Colin's invariable face in order to clearly remind him that I need to approve any changes he wants to make, *before* they're in process, and that I, the owner, should be paying for said changes. "What if you fall off a ladder or crush your finger?" I asked him.

He seemed to understand for a few weeks, during which time he put in a dimmer switch for the chandelier, installed more track lighting, and beautifully painted yet another room, all with my prior knowledge. I congratulated myself for facing the problem and Colin for responding in kind. But now the conversation has again slowed. I rarely see him, but I can hear him—hammering, sawing, drilling; working away on something. He has taken the doors off the kitchen cabinets, and though my recon access is limited in that part of the house, I believe he is testing several paint colors to redo them. My nighttime creeper moments (he really should get some curtains) now reveal that he's created a huge mosaic-like collage of colored plastic or paper squares that covers the entire wall above the mantel. He's putting in new (supposedly removable?) flooring on top of the old painted wood planks in his room. I shit you not: he has built a squirrel lounge in his window frame, a wood panel with a squirrel-sized round hole on one side and a glass panel on the interior for observing, ant-farm style. Inside the box he has placed batting for the squirrels' comfort; so far the animals are a no-show.

At this point the room is about 55 percent old hotel, 40 percent tech startup, 5 percent squirrel residence, if you're keeping score.

The guy's got a good eye; I admit it. That doesn't alter the fact that this apartment is home to two young men, with their attendant piles of clothes and dirty dishes and some less-than-appealing smells. But it's sunny, well-decorated, and feels cared for. I still don't feel totally recognized by Colin as the actual owner of the house, but I would rather have a tenant who cares about improving his surroundings than one who lives among his own refuse.

Colin is awkward; he is a leisurely, sporadically employed enigma. He is candid about dealing with mental illness. I like Colin, although I cannot claim to know what makes him tick. He's smart and appears older than he is. He's curious and introspective and slightly problematic. He has surprised me by turning over a rather outgoing new leaf. We carry on actual conversations now, voluntary ones, good ones, about Trump and the strange, terrible state of America and the brilliance of Samantha Bee. He has adopted a highly sociable black cat he named Joe Biden, but whom everyone else calls Buster. Under Colin's care, Buster has gone from skinny and sniffling to large and glossy. He greets me in the driveway when I come home, and he visits me in my apartment, napping on the couch like he owns the place.

If I am to present a well-rounded portrait of Colin, though, I must discuss his car, for Colin is the car; the car is Colin. The car is a hulking, green, 2000-era Volvo wagon with various mechanical problems. The car's metamorphosis began when Colin discovered a way to print custom bumper stickers one at a time, with stark white letters on a black background. His car soon became a tribute to his favorite comedians, authors, and thinkers, whose names reverently graced the bumper: Patrice O'Neal, Bill Hicks, Dave Chappelle, James Baldwin, Friedrich Nietzsche, Leo Tolstoy. Later, perhaps having received some flak for his all-male pantheon, he threw a bone to the ladies and added Tina Fey. He topped it off with a Bernie 2016 and a Black Lives Matter. At this point, the car got him some notice around town (I mean, a *Leo Tolstoy bumper sticker?*), with people leaving him notes and giving him hand salutes of one kind or another. An acquaintance in town spotted his car parked somewhere and found it so ludicrous she posted a photo of it on Instagram. One of the commenters noted that they "saw this narc wagon parked outside the police station."

So a few months pass, and Colin gets to thinking that this level of ornamentation was a good first step, but the #narcwagon is not confrontational enough. He begins to reimagine the car as a sort of performance art piece, a way to start a conversation that he is not self-possessed enough to have face-to-face.

The previous stickers are removed and replaced with a single Black Lives Matter sticker (banner, really) the width of the bumper and twice as tall. Then the same sticker appears on the side of the car; this one is maybe four feet long. And so on and so forth, until no matter from which angle you look at the car, a huge Black Lives Matter banner is visible.

So Colin—who is white, should you need confirmation—begins driving this car around Providence and Rhode Island. He gets plenty of thumbs-up and words of encouragement. But he also gets into angry scrapes with some jacked-up, hate-filled white guys. A couple of dudes in trucks casually try to run him off the road. And, of course, he regularly gets the bird.

A technophile with spare time, Colin has now installed cameras all over his car so that he can park it in various locations and observe people's reactions. He has put a solar panel on the roof to power the cameras. (He is often to be spotted in the driveway drilling holes in the roof of his car.) He's installed the least threatening-sounding car alarm ever made—it makes a cute, bumbling *blooooop, blooooop* sound. Colin is trying to decide what to do with the cam footage. He's kicking around a few ideas for extending the car-as-political-conversation-starter concept, including—and he admits this needs some work—another banner reading "A Vehicle for Social Change."

I don't know how to feel about all of this. On one hand, I can appreciate Colin stepping out of his socially-awkward-white-guy comfort zone to publicly support a crucially important movement. But the very fact that he is able to do this so boldly and ostentatiously, using his suburbanesque Volvo for Christ's sake, is an effect of his tremendous privilege. I think he knows it and feels he's pushing boundaries.

I feel uncomfortable just backing this car out of the driveway to park it on the street, and not just because it smells like old burritos and Play-Doh; being inside this moving statement makes a person extremely visible, as if you are representing the movement itself; let me tell you, neither I nor Colin have any business doing that. I'm just not sure that black people, the people in full charge of the movement, really want to see the galvanizing civil rights statement of this decade writ large on some white guy's car. Does it help anything at all, in even the most miniscule way? Or is he co-opting Black Lives Matter for the hell of it, experimenting with something that doesn't belong to him?

Colin lives with a fair amount of luxury—enough that he can do pretty much whatever he wants, whenever he wants. He doesn't need to police his expression, because in our society he is unlikely to be victimized or incriminated for any of what he says. His ongoing comfort is not at issue. But he does try, and he does care. He could sit back, deflect pangs of anger and helplessness, and "avoid politics" like the many similarly privileged people who wait quietly for our societal unrest to blow over. It's necessary to accept that hate and conflict are, in a sense, America's default condition. Colin's method of publicly confronting that may need serious refinement, but at least he's out there.

Economies of Scale

Our childhood homes set off a lifetime of comparisons. They confine us in loaded symbolism, becoming the first places we know down to the cracks in the walls and the faded spots in the carpet. We mark every new address against our previous homes, based on the ease or difficulty of living there, the tenderness and toil of our home-based relationships, the memories we later seek to duplicate or to avoid. I came to PennHenge with a variety of comparative impressions intact and each one of my tenants over the years has brought his or her own.

For roughly the first half of my life, "home" meant a small town, a small house, and a small family. It was an insular life, and I was both thrilled and afraid to break out of it as soon as I made it to adulthood.

In buying PennHenge, I wanted to preserve the stability of my childhood, the sense that all was well, that we as a family had it mostly together. I thought that buying a big house and living in it with a big crew would keep me ultrasocial, keep me from retreating into progressively tinier spheres as my parents had, while settling me into a self-sufficient routine as I, the Lady in Charge, happily managed the house's needs. Only later did it occur to me that the path I'd picked led away from reliable routine and toward constant upheaval. And that sometimes, being social in my home would have to mean living with erratic people.

My parents are the most practical people I have ever known. They have been ruthless savers for their entire lives, working hard at ill-paying, depressing jobs and being so strenuously frugal that they were able to retire earlier than they had planned, to a Florida-snowbird-condo situation no less. Back in their days of financial uncertainty and anxiety, though, when life stretched out ahead of them—a minefield of potential expenses to be evaded with deft penny-pinching moves—they did something that would befuddle most modern thirty-year-olds. They knew they couldn't afford a classic suburban single-family house, but they didn't want to be renters when I came into the world, so they bought a two-bedroom mobile home, which sat on rented land in a park of some 125 prefab aluminum-sided castles on wheels. Thusly, I spent my childhood in a trailer park.

SOUTH DRIVE

Rows of multicolored trailers, parked vertically to maximize space, lined up dutifully along each of Sunny Acres's six streets. Some trailers were decorated and landscaped to the nines; others stood starkly on brown grass as if they'd dropped out of the sky. Some had sunrooms and patios and swing sets. The place was clean and orderly enough, and there was a big grassy field at the top of the hill by a busy road for the kids to run around in. There was a hierarchy to the layout: North Drive, which was just a single street connecting to the main road, was exclusively for old folks. South Drive was a mix of families and retirees. There were four side streets. You guessed it: First St., Second St., Third St., Fourth St., all of which spilled out from one side of South Drive. These side streets had smaller, cheaper lots and a few spindly trees and shrubs. We had a delicate little dogwood that my mom loved.

Halloween was the best time to be a kid at Sunny Acres. Besides the clear delight many of its residents took in decorating—lights, sound effects, animatronics, dry ice, apple-bobbing barrels—it was the bang-per-buck candy-hoarding capital of the county. In two hours, you could hit up every trailer and end your night with a full garbage bag (or three pillowcases, if you were the wimpy type who had to go home and unload periodically so as to carry it all).

Sunny Acres—which my parents nicknamed "Belly Achers"—was a microcosm of society. There was a little of everything, humanity-wise, tightly crammed within its bounds. There were upstanding folks stuck in the relentless daily grind and struggling mightily to pay the bills; there were sourpuss retirees who bickered and drank their dwindling days away; there were sweet grandmas who offered me fun-size Snickers and root beer on my walk home from the bus stop; there were quiet, defeated people for whom divorce, illness, loss, and other personal calamities had limited their ambitions; there were big-fish narcissists who spontaneously combusted into spectacular displays of drama, exploiting the insular nature of the park by creating their own fiefdoms within it. There was one thing just about everyone under seventy-five had in common at Sunny Acres, though: a desire to get out. Although it wasn't a slum by any means, it felt like a place from which very little good could come. It was a place of resignation. If you had any life left in you at all, you didn't want to live it there.

The trailer itself was built at a kid-friendly scale and had a kind of zany 1970s color scheme and style. It was covered in brown wall-to-wall carpeting and yellow linoleum, with Formica countertops and faux stone and wood paneling on the walls. I thought it was cool that I lived in a technically portable metallic capsule. I liked sprawling on my white pleather beanbag chair in front of the TV or cozily chatting with my parents. I liked sleeping in my twin bed with the streetlight shining down through the window. Still, there was no covering up the fact that our dwelling wasn't fancy: all of the surfaces had a paper-thinness to them. We were jammed in close enough to hear the neighbors' TVs. And we were the first in town to be evacuated when there was a big storm or hurricane bearing down, lest our little free-floating palaces drift out to sea.

My flower-wallpapered bedroom was in front, next to the street, and contained my bed (complete with railings, because I used to tumble out of it), a dresser my grandfather had made, a school desk, a bookshelf for my precious Little Miss and Little Golden Books, and my very favorite place, a triangle-shaped closet that I would hang out in so frequently that my parents installed a light to help me read in comfort. Then there was the living room, with its little TV cart, flowered couch, and wood stove; then the kitchen and a diminutive dining room that had been built later as part of a fancy addition. The bathroom (more flowered wallpaper) was next; and in the back, my parents' tiny bedroom. It was a place ideally built for compactness, for small, efficient people like the Warner family.

My family specialized in minding our own business, and gregariousness wasn't an attribute to be especially valued. Being an only child, too, I learned early how to properly be alone. I played at adult occupations: I was a doctor, a shopkeeper, a secretary, a writer, an artist, setting up elaborate "offices" and answering "phones" authoritatively. I never felt lonely; I never wished for a sibling (though it might be nice to have one now). Instead, those long and uninterrupted afternoons of play—dinner simmering away in the slow cooker and my parents keeping an ear toward me but letting me do my thing—felt quietly joyful. I observed the chaos at my friends' houses—siblings tearing each other apart on the regular—and I only felt sorry for them.

When I did have to be around other kids, though, they usually took my calmness for weakness, and I was roundly pushed around. My arm still cracks from the time the monstrous Jenny F. wrestled me off the top bar of the swing set. Despite my shyness and the occasional mistreatment I received at the hands of the bigger, older, cooler, tougher girls on the street, I made a few friends at the trailer park—kids whose families always seemed to be splintered, dysfunctional, disheveled, overpopulated, broke, or some combination thereof. When I started going to school, I was surprised and a little seduced by the air of virtuosity and wealth wafting from my classmates' parents.

My hometown of Portsmouth, Rhode Island, is an island burg of just under twenty thousand people (93 percent of whom are white), where in 2012 the median household income was around $75,000 and the median home value was over $345,000. If there's one place dragging down that average, friends, it's Sunny Acres and the other trailer park in town, where, as my mom would say, the folks "don't have two nickels to rub together." Being a kid from the trailer park in a town of rich kids perfecting late-twentieth-century entitlement—in close proximity to rich and hallowed Newport—let me know where I stood, and it wasn't at the top, or even the middle. Forever hopping back and forth between observing the rarified lives of my schoolmates (BMWs, sprawling houses, equestrian lessons, ski vacations) and returning to my own reality (Datsuns, dog houses, episodes of *Welcome Back, Kotter*, trips to Kmart), I was aware of status as soon as I hit public school. I never believed I'd own anything, much less that I deserved to. I worried about my future: who would give me a job, someday? How would I navigate life, when everybody I knew already seemed to have more than us? Adulthood looked treacherous, fraught with drudgery like paying taxes, working late, getting the car fixed, and cleaning the toilet, and if you did any of it wrong, you would be arrested and thrown in the slammer.

SILVA AVENUE

As a result of their relentless economizing, my parents got us out of Sunny Acres when I was ten. They bought a small, lifeless three-bedroom ranch house a few miles down the road, in a quiet neighborhood of simple suburban houses just off one of the two main roads in town. I remember their relief upon moving in, despite the fact that the house needed work. There must have been a saturation point for them with the trailer park, as there may someday be with me and my house—a point at which the annoyances and the little indignities become too much, and you clutch your tiny nest egg and say screw it, peace out.

Bland and ordinary as the place was, it was our house, a place where our little triad could prosper. The house was shabby, but not falling apart. Over our first few years living there, my parents got right to work painting, putting in new floors and carpeting, staining cabinets and doors, replacing the old windows. My mom painted every room a utilitarian, dispassionate white, which my dad said was like "living in an aspirin tablet." The house feels close—there are a lot of walls that a more adventurous homeowner might alter or tear down. The overall interior effect is of a series of small, white boxes—

none of the six rooms is much larger than any of the others.

It makes some sense that I didn't love the house, at first, as much as I'd loved the trailer—I missed the unconventional layout of the trailer and the snugness of my closet lair. I missed the trailer's crank windows and how they swung open from the bottom. I missed the few friends I'd had back at Sunny Acres. There were only a couple of kids in the new neighborhood, which abutted a loud, traffic-clogged road. I was bordering on my teenage years and prone to the attendant aloofness and snobbery. But I started to come around. This house did have something that the trailer didn't: a basement. I cranked my boom box, laced up my roller skates (white leather with fat orange wheels), and cruised that smooth-ass concrete for all it was worth. Sometimes I invited my new friend Andrea, who lived across the street, to join me. Upstairs, another perk: blessedly free access to MTV in its late-eighties glory days, a gift from the basic cable gods. I wore a spot into the carpet in front of the TV, finally getting the pop culture education I desperately wanted, and just in time to prep me for high school.

My bedroom was one of the aforementioned white cubes; it had a ceiling fan and two small windows in the corner that faced the road at the back of the house. The closet was too small to inhabit, and I guess by the time I was twelve, I was over that. I had a plywood desk in the corner with a frustrating pre-internet ultra-low-memory Smith-Corona word processor perched upon it, and a couple of bookshelves to house my radio, favorite paperbacks, and a small collection of CDs. As I got a bit older, I commandeered my dad's old Zenith turntable, with its cool cone-shaped speakers, and started buying records at yard sales for a dime or a quarter each. I was a religious listener of American Top 40 with Casey Kasem, and I loved the pop music of the time: Madonna and Prince and Roxette and Neneh Cherry. But I was also in love with sixties and seventies rock and topped off my room decor with posters of *Jim Morrison: An American Poet*, as well as my ultimate obsession, my homeboys Led Zeppelin. Weekends, I'd sleep over at my friend Lisa's; we'd watch our worn VHS copy of *Led Zeppelin: The Song Remains the Same* that we'd split the cost of, and she'd fall asleep while I'd stay gloriously awake and fantasize about being born twenty years earlier so I could see this overwrought spectacle in the flesh, so I could sway and bathe in the languid ink-blue light of 1973 at Madison Square Garden. The boys at school were so dumb. Give me Jimmy Page! Lisa and I read in *Hammer of the Gods: The Led Zeppelin Saga* by Stephen Davis that Page dated a fourteen-year-old in the early 1970s; far from being horrified, in our cluelessness we figured it meant we had a chance.

But I don't think I was Jimmy's type. Until adolescence, when my mom took pity on me and bought me a single pair of contact lenses—which I wore until they were ripped and infectiously dirty, fearing the parental rebuff associated with asking for a replacement pair—I sported grandma glasses that obstructed half of my face. My clothes were bought off the clearance rack at the Sears outlet or TJ Maxx. I was short and thin, with brown hair and brown eyes. I blended into the crowd, staying fairly neutral other than my baggy, black classic rock T-shirts. As the girls around me started to get curvy, grow boobs, and face the sexual scrutiny of their peers, I hunkered down in my pseudo pupal stage, inhabiting a gawky middle ground of having dire crushes on boys, acting tough and uninterested anyway, and then going home to play with my Barbies.

The summer I turned fifteen, my best friend called to ask if I wanted to work a catering job at the exclusive prep school where her dad had the very official title of Business Manager. The pay was fifty dollars—half a *year's* worth of my abysmal two-dollar allowance. As soon as I saw that check with my name on it, I was hooked. The type of work was beside the point—I would have done any job with equal enthusiasm—I just wanted to bust out and make my own money.

Shortly after that first one-off work day, I was offered a regular spot on the schedule, working in the dining hall after school and on weekends. I was going to be a lunch lady. (The official job title was "server," but tellingly, the only people who had that title were women. Let's just go with "lunch lady.")

The lunch lady is not a particularly admired or well-loved archetype. She is an object of pity and ridicule, tasked with slinging food of questionable provenance at little punks for whom sassing her is a competitive sport. Her greatest skill is portion control, whereby she can save the institution a few pennies by making her ice cream scoops of mashed potatoes a smidge less plentiful.

It wasn't sexy, but it was my new job; it paid $5.50 an hour (the minimum wage in Rhode Island at the time was $4.45), and I was going to embrace it. I was in the strange position of being the same age as the crowd I was serving; depending on which kid was next in line, this could be fun or it could be embarrassing and dehumanizing. These kids made my public-school friends look budget. They were the children of famous artists, of liquor barons, of corporate CEOs, and they smelled like a whole other echelon of wealth I didn't even know existed. One kid ever so helpfully let me know that I should give him as much food as he wanted, because "my parents pay your salary." Harsh them-and-us differences were in high relief. Luckily, though, it was the dawn of the age of grunge, and my work style—typically a thrifted flannel shirt over my company-issue polo shirt, stretchy black skirt, striped knee socks, and china doll Mary Janes—was quite au courant, other than the lame polo. Designer labels were out, tatters and rips were in, so we all looked about the same.

I wrapped up my last two years of high school with waning enthusiasm. My classes were not the problem—it was the people around me. My class was full of overachievers with an annoyingly high level of school spirit—people who simultaneously got stellar grades, showed up for everything, ran track, killed it in academic decathlon, and drank and smoked all weekend. I just could not hang. I judged them all, unkindly, hating their perkiness beyond any reason.

I found the pockets of freaks—theater, chorus, literary magazine—and I uneasily stuck myself in with them. I did well in school, but I was nowhere near the top of the class. I got a scholarship to the state university and committed to go there, if only to avoid student loans.

School sucked; my real friends were at work. The work itself may have been mindless, but my two best girlfriends worked there with me, and we made everything into a joke. We stuck maxi pads on the wall in the ladies' bathroom; we snuck out bottles of nasty white wine in our backpacks; we put hot sauce in each other's cups of Coke; we dabbed sour cream on the earpiece of the phone, and then yelled, "Phone's for you!" to whichever cook was on duty. There was a troop of slightly older skater guys who worked there as dishwashers and who we were always falling all over ourselves to impress. They listened to punk cassettes in their food-scrap-covered work area and skated on the loading dock during break time. They flung hot dishrags at us and openly ogled our knee-sock-clad legs when we sauntered by, trying to look as fetching as possible while carrying thirty-pound boxes of cream cheese. Some making out took place among the juice machines and in the back of the storeroom. It was a disgusting, charged, slightly abusive, often unsupervised workplace, the kind of job that sounded perfectly fine to Mom, but was actually a haven for indulging all the bad bits of our budding personalities.

As we finished high school, both of my best friends left for college and new adventures. Kurt Cobain and Jerry Garcia died, Bill Clinton *may* have had sex with that woman in the Oval Office, and it felt like a listless new era. I was officially enrolled at the University of Rhode Island, which had recently been voted the number one party school in the country. A born commuter, I lived at home and appeared on campus in my parentally funded Honda ten minutes before my first class, promptly zipping back toward the exit ten minutes after my last class. The campus was filled with obnoxious, white-hatted frat boys who were just getting into Dave Matthews Band and the local hell-on-earth jam band, Foxtrot Zulu. In my giant Minor Threat T-shirt, ripped jeans, and skate shoes, and with a calculated perma-scowl on my face, I let them know that I did not want to party, did not want to get to know them, did not want their sexual attention.

After a year of commuting from my parents' house, I took my eighty-two-dollar-a-week lunch lady paycheck, teamed up with three friends (two of whom worked with me), and rounded up an apartment. In a sign of how much I adored college life, the apartment was fifteen minutes further away from school than my parents' home, meaning I had a commute of over an hour each way. But the apartment was $500 a month, and split four ways that meant all I had to do was swing a very quaint $125 a month. My parents let me know in no uncertain terms that I wouldn't be getting their help with groceries, books, or gas, but they'd still pay the insurance on my car. I was not permitted to bring my laundry home or store any stuff in the basement. Once I moved out, I wouldn't be coming back. Although they were probably just being tough with me, and would have helped had I fallen way behind, I wanted to show them that I was independent and could shoulder all of the work and school and financial responsibility by myself. I never asked them for a thing. Still haven't.

ROMA STREET

The new apartment I shared with my besties— Heather, Erin, and Samantha—was a third-floor three-bedroom (we made the living room into one more), not dissimilar to the one I live in now, in a triple-decker probably built in the 1930s. The kitchen was in the center, the three bedrooms in a row on one side. There was a pantry with big, old cupboards and a small tiled bathroom. A wooden porch ran across the front of the house. The sole source of warmth was a clunky gas heater in the kitchen, and with all the bedroom doors closed, in the winter the temperature differential was fierce enough that I wore multiple layers and a hat to bed.

We decorated with whatever we all brought from home, plus found trash-night furniture and the occasional thrift or yard sale score. Heather's dad, an artist and class-A scavenger, unearthed trinkets and old signs for us to decorate with. All four of us were in school, and we all had jobs, so the apartment was a beehive of women rushing in and out, casting off outfits and wiggling into new ones, gulping down bowls of cereal and checking the answering machine. When we could scrounge a little down time, we would make crafts, watch *90210*, go dancing, discuss our love for Deee-Lite and Björk, and stage impromptu photo shoots in which we'd dress in our favorite seventies-era clothes and fall into our best sweet/hot nineties poses on a secondhand futon.

Despite the multitudes of college boys seemingly at our disposal, only Samantha dated men from school. The rest of us chose from the same extremely limited pool of skater/musician/ne'er-do-well dudes we'd known and/or worked with for years, who to their credit were exponentially more fun and adventurous than the featureless human lumps at school.

Bristol, Rhode Island, the little town we lived in, has since been condo-ized and made upscale, but it was a classic New England fishing village then: a picturesque place characterized by stunning old houses, factories on the waterfront, and boats clanging on the docks. It was beautiful and scrappy; I loved its high-end/low-end duality. I was enamored with having everything I needed—the bank, the post office, the library, the bakery, the liquor store—within ten minutes' walk. Our house was in the most crowded section of town, a jumble of skinny one-way streets with tenement houses packed in about as closely as they are in Federal Hill. Most of the neighbors were of Portuguese or Italian extraction; accordingly, you couldn't throw a rock without hitting a church, bakery, or butcher shop. Although I was only fifteen minutes from my parents' house, Bristol felt infinitely more present, more alive to me.

After a year or so in that first apartment, Heather

came home one night and said, "There's an apartment for rent in the boys' building." The "boys" were
four of the dudes from our little crowd—all of whom
we had some sort of history with—and their building
was a cute duplex right in "downtown" Bristol. Her
current boyfriend lived there, and so did Erin's, so
needless to say, they were on board. I was worried
about the *huge* rent increase—this place was $650
per month, meaning I would be on the hook for $162
every month. That forty-dollar difference was eight
hours of work and half a paycheck. But the apartment was adorable, the location was perfect, and
we'd be a united front of coolness in the building. It
was intolerably cute: boys on one side, girls on the
other. We gave notice to our sweet, elderly landlady
and packed up.

HOPE STREET

We four felt very adult upon moving into our new,
slightly tonier apartment; we wouldn't need to re-
purpose any rooms to make bedrooms, and it had a
big kitchen and living room. Our new landlord was
an elderly lawyer everyone called the Judge; his
building management style was sufficiently hands-
off that he allowed us to paint the kitchen a tremendous shade of salmon that I can recall today with
extreme clarity. The apartment was on two levels:
Erin and Samantha's bedrooms were downstairs, off
the kitchen, and Heather and I were on the upper
level, at the top of a squeaky, narrow set of stairs;

we shared a huge walk-in closet that was centered between our two linoleum-floored, attic-style rooms. My room was narrow and its sloping ceiling contained a single skylight window, under which I put up a shelf and installed a few spindly plants. My desk and the Smith-Corona word processing torture device went into a dark, vortex-like corner, from which I wrote the million-and-one papers that stood between me and finishing college at last; my bed went directly under the skylight, with a dresser and TV at its foot. My trusty bookshelf, loaded down by now, was by the door. I tacked up a poster of Björk and my favorite yard sale art, arranged my CDs and records, and settled in.

Though we all spent plenty of time cloistered in our rooms, upon flinging open our doors there was a ready-made party just outside. The liquor store was next door. We often climbed out the kitchen window and sat on the little patch of roof overlooking the street, yelling at passersby, smoking, clutching beers, listening to Black Flag or Misfits. Our house was a stop for the local high school kids who walked around aimlessly in the afternoons; they'd stop by with their skateboards and sit on our stoop or come inside and bug us. It was a welcoming place, and a good-natured one, not nearly as depraved as it could have been.

After a couple of years of idyllic young adult fun there, though, suddenly I couldn't muster up much excitement for the place. I was in a relationship with a brooding small-town guy who was friends with the whole crowd at the house, and it had become miserable. He was bitter about my going to (and imminently graduating from) college, more annoyed than supportive of any limited successes I had, and he seemed to want to keep me closer and closer to home. I had a visceral reaction to that; although I was rather passive as a girlfriend then, I knew when something was the wrong thing.

I broke up with him, dragging it out because I didn't know how to do it, and his insecurities flared. First, he threatened to jump off the bridge, then he threatened to hang himself. Once he realized he wouldn't be able to stop me from leaving with intimations of self-harm, he started coming after me. He grinningly held me down on the bed and choked me. He stole my keys to keep me immobile, and then mentally tortured me, begging me to come back and using rote abusive man-speak like, "If I can't have you, no one will." I once caught him trying to get onto the roof to peer into my room through the skylight.

Everyone in the house knew what was going on, though they probably didn't know the extent of it. I wanted to keep it private, out of a childish embarrassment and pride. When it would spill out into the open, friends would ask him to leave, tell him he was out of line, vaguely take my side. Heather told him off pretty effectively a few times. I don't think my housemates knew day-to-day whether we were patching things up, or whether I was frantically trying to get away from him. Though I knew it was the latter, I didn't ask for help.

A few weeks later, at a show, I met James. Our first date was on my twenty-first birthday. He was off-the-charts intelligent, he was funny, he was moody and sarcastic, he was in a band. We got close quickly, and he was justifiably incensed that Other Dude was still bothering me. James came to the house, playing it cool, and when Other Dude showed up, James utterly dismantled him with words. I never saw Other Dude again.

James's rather valiant move made us an official united front and cemented us into coupledom. It also drew me away from my housemates, because the "guy side" of the house thought James had overstepped. My loyalties had changed. The next spring, both of us still dreamy-eyed and writing poetry about the other, we planned to get an apartment in Providence. I was ready. I was done with this little incestuous pocket of small-town living. I was finally going to quit my dumb dining hall job and be an adult, in an adult relationship, with an adult job and a city apartment.

SHELDON STREET

In June, as a promising new summer unfolded, James and I loaded up his van full of my stuff, and we rolled slowly away from Bristol, coming up a half hour later on the east side of Providence. The air in June in this part of Providence has a characteristic odd but not unpleasant smell that is something like low tide plus melted tires plus freshly unfurled leaves. I sniffed it greedily as I stepped down from the van. As mentioned, the previous art-school tenants were still sleeping in the apartment when we arrived—fresh-faced and *ready for our new lives, please*—so we had to wait it out a day or so as they dragged themselves up and out. When they'd finally vacated, a trail of their stuff was left behind.

My favorite thing about this fusty apartment was the red, curved entry door at street level. It was exquisite, although it encouraged higher expectations of the interior than the place could fulfill. Our apartment was on the second and third floors, and the entrance was in the living room, which we sloppily painted a confrontational shade of red, accentuated by a blue-green area rug that James brought. The couch—an awful peachy color and rigidly shaped—was found on the street. A fourteen-inch TV sat on a wooden cube, with an ornate seventies-style lamp on a green table. An old Indian tapestry—a coveted object purchased by James's recently deceased, much-missed dad—hung framed on the wall. There was no space in the kitchen for a table, so we put one near the back wall, at least *near* the kitchen. The room was dark, strange, and had a patchwork quality to it. Somehow it worked for us—although apparently not for anyone else: later, when potential renters came to look at the apartment, they gasped audibly, and someone said breathlessly, "We'd be able to paint this, right?!"

The kitchen was a sort of hallway with a window at the end, and it had all of the necessities jammed in. I've heard this phrase uttered about many Providence apartments, and it was absolutely true of Sheldon Street: "No matter how much you scrub, it never gets clean." A fine grit was ground into every surface: the sink, the ancient wood flooring, the black tile countertop. There was a tiny closet of a bathroom just off the kitchen, with a water-hogging old toilet and a shower stall.

Up the stairs was our bedroom, a large room with a wood floor so chipped and decayed that we once lost our pet ferret for a few hours as she wriggled into a hole and crawled around under it, trailing dust bunnies on her whiskers when she returned. The windows were drafty, but the heat worked. Our mattress went directly on the floor. James's computer went into the next room, which was sort of an office/guest room hybrid. That room looked out over the landlord's very attractive landscaped grounds below, which James definitely puked on once.

The landlord was cool, if a bit hands-off. He was absolutely overwhelmed—and I can relate—by owning this big house and dealing with us and his first-floor tenant. Or I should say he was overwhelmed by his tenants, plus the maintenance of his own gorgeous section of the house, which contained two smart and high-achieving kids under twelve. He and his wife were lovely, and they cared enough to listen to James and me opine on various topics. I was jazzed to be in this apartment; I was also worried, because the rent was $800 per month. This was almost two and a half times what I paid at the last place, which to be fair had been an utter steal, even for twenty years ago. I had to cross the threshold to a full-time job.

I bought myself an Interview Dress and made

the rounds. It wasn't long before I rounded up a job writing resumes for a career counseling outfit, at ten dollars an hour, full time. Strangely, I was the only employee other than my boss, the owner of the company. The office consisted of the front two rooms of my boss's condo. If he was around, I was forced to listen to the local light-rock station (a special kind of torture reserved for the already-demeaned office worker). If he left for an appointment or errand, it was just me and Tootsie, an enormous white cockatoo that was the light of his life. Tootsie stared at me from her cage—unyieldingly, all day, every day. Once, when my boss was away, she somehow got out of her cage, climbed up to the top of it, and sat there squawking, moving rhythmically and talking at me while I, frozen, weighed whether to make a run for it, get under my desk earthquake-style, or do nothing at all. *Was she jealous of me?* I wondered. *Angry? And could her beak snap my forearm in half?* Finally, my boss ambled in, tsk'd her, and put her back in her cage. I smiled weakly, my hands shaking. I hated my job.

Though my boss was a fair guy who gave me little raises and bonuses whenever he could, I knew my days there were numbered. Other than observing the machinations of Tootsie, there was *no* action at this job. I would receive summaries of people's work experience on a written form or by email; sometimes I would meet them and have a short conversation. Then I would write their resumes and several variations on the same formulaic cover letter. My mornings were spent hating on "Black Velvet" by

Alannah Myles while daydreaming about lunch and a car nap; my afternoons were spent hating on Seal's "Kiss from a Rose" while daydreaming about watching TV with our elderly coon cat, Elvis, eating a cheap vegan dinner, and sending James off to his grinding third-shift job as a graphic designer for an auto classifieds magazine. On Sunday nights, I would cry just thinking about starting another week at my job. It was no way to live.

We made it work for exactly one year.

COMMONWEALTH AVENUE

All I remember about the two guys who rented me and James our first apartment in Boston was that one of them was named Donald, and he chain-smoked and looked like a wizened old-school detective. They worked out of a thickly nicotine-stained, fake wood-paneled office above a pizza parlor on the Boston University campus. Like their office, the apartment they rented to us was of another time; at $850 a month, it was literally the cheapest above-ground non-rent-controlled one-bedroom within the city proper. It was on the first floor of a sagging, red stucco-fronted building of perhaps twelve apartments in the ugly epicenter of student housing in Boston, equidistant between Boston University and Boston College.

The living room was big enough to have a TV watching zone and an office zone, which was novel. It also had bizarre built-in white wooden cabinetry along the entire length of the interior wall—rows of huge cabinets with doors, which were great for stashing anything we didn't want to look at. In the center of these cabinets, there was a large mirror with 1940s-style cut-out woodwork all around it, almost like a vanity setup for an old-time lady to do her rollers or her makeup. It was so large and ornate that it made no sense in this little railroad apartment, and I think it's the only reason the place wasn't snapped up well before we got there. No self-respecting frat boy could look at this every day, and it was way out of style, decor-wise, for a design fetishist to live with.

The bathroom was a sea green tiled job, again with an overabundance of cabinets. Everything in it was original to the building when we moved in, until the toilet broke and was replaced and the old sea green one sat morosely behind the building for months. The bedroom was a basic white cube, but the floors were nice, and it was very cozy due to the landlord-controlled heat, which was cranked so high we had to open the windows in January.

The kitchen, well, the kitchen was a bit of a bummer. It had more of that white cut-out woodwork and a gruesome brown linoleum floor. Moving in, we opened the gigantic 1960s Frigidaire, which had been left unplugged, to find a desiccated, moldy ice cream cake in the freezer. Elvis's litter box seemed awkward no matter where we put it, so it ended up in a corner of the kitchen. Only problem was, Elvis was so old that he couldn't poop in the box anymore; he'd get in, hang his butt off the side, and poop on the floor instead. Returning from work often meant encountering the noxious remnants in the kitchen, mere feet away from human food. This kitchen was also interesting because every once in a while, someone we didn't know would literally stumble in through the poorly secured back door to the building; James would usher these drunk people out, mostly kindly.

This was my first time living in a building whose landlord I would never meet— *couldn't* meet, in fact, even if I wanted to. He had hired a management company, as these guys did, and spoke his veiled communications through them only. When Donald from the agency would call us, he'd refer to the landlord, in his hushed Boston accent, as "Mistah Kantos." What was this, a James Bond code name? Anyway, mostly we just wrote checks to Mr. Kantos, rarely requiring his assistance. Only when raw sewage bubbled up into our bathroom sink, or when water started coming through our kitchen ceiling because the tenants upstairs had forgotten to shut off their faucet—only then did we deign to disturb Donald and, by extension, Mistah Kantos.

I had my adult-ish life and my biggish-city apartment, but felt restless. I was struggling to do well at my first editorial job; James started art school and within a few weeks decided it was a stupid waste of money for someone like him. He instead got a job at a web/video/graphic design startup, which sounded like an enormously lucky break, but they could barely pay the bills, payroll included. We had almost no one to hang out with, and the shine was just beginning to come off of our relationship, the love poetry phase having long since ended. I applied to grad school, planning to keep working full-time to keep my loans at a minimum, if I got in. I was stacking the deck against myself, pushing to work ever harder and put aside all of the rest.

MORAINE STREET

This was the last apartment we lived in before I bought the house, the place with the five male roommates and all their many wayward pubes; the place that launched the whole discussion of going back to Providence and buying PennHenge. These landlords, too, were elsewhere—they were rumored to be in New York—and Ted, the friendly but ineffectual property manager, kept things more or less in working condition.

Our place was in a sweet two-family house in the middle of what has since become the wildly gentrified neighborhood of Jamaica Plain in Boston. Moraine Street was friendly, with a communal, hippie vibe, and was just beginning to be the kind of place where every house had a Prius in the driveway and a double-wide stroller parked in the mudroom. We had a big tree in front of the house, and a few more behind, so it always felt shady and languid, protected from the worst of summer's heat and noise. The wood door frames and trim had never been painted; they were stained darkly and made the interior feel serious, library-like. There was a white tiled kitchen and two porches—one just outside the kitchen and another small one off the third floor that was my personal "do not talk to me" zone. There were three bedrooms on the second floor and three on the third. My own room was on the upper level; it was long and narrow and had a slanted ceiling, so I could only stand up fully within a slim slice of the room. I jammed a hand-me-down midcentury desk in a corner, and put my bed in the center, rigged up a box fan to fit into the skylight above the bed, put my little TV at the end of the bed, and threw some clothes into a bureau. James and I slept in this room, but he had his own room downstairs, where he drew, and where he'd sit until 3:00 a.m. at his huge desktop Power Mac G4.

The separation had already begun. We just didn't know it yet.

I started grad school the same year we moved into Moraine Street, and I was still working full time. I was gunning it—for exactly what, I couldn't have told you, but I knew I could and would work harder than the next lady or guy. In a parody of collegiate exhaustion, I fell asleep on a book almost every night. My celiac symptoms were kicking into high gear, though I was years from seeking any kind of treatment. I read on the bus, on the subway, during my lunch breaks at work. I nodded off on the bus coming home from night classes. I loved it; I hated it. I felt alive; I felt hollow. James was irritable; he rightly complained about my packed schedule and the fact that we rarely did anything together. I pretty much said, "Tough shit. This is something I need to do. I know it sucks. It'll be over in a year." Delayed gratification was my modus operandi, and I forced him to live with it, too.

This was the state of affairs when, upon my finishing grad school, James and I nearly immediately began talking about moving, and then quickly about buying a house. None of the introspection that should have accompanied such a decision came close to happening. Instead, we stuffed down our uncertainties and burgeoning unhappiness and we decided to do the next thing, and do it now.

PENN STREET

I don't blame Mistah Kantos and the Boston landlords for hiring professionals to handle their tenants; there's a big difference between living in and managing my three-family house, and running a twelve-unit building or multiple properties in another state. It would be unfair of me to expect other landlords to oversee everything in their buildings, the way I'm able to. But I will say this: I take a personal interest because it's my home, not my profession. I don't want to build a characterless aspirin-tablet empire. I don't care about maximizing my dollars, about raising rents and getting off without doing much.

Someday, when I leave PennHenge—and who knows when that will be—I hope that whomever ends up with it can see that however weird it is, however kaleidoscopic the paint job, however out of control the decor, however overgrown the backyard, I loved this absurd house and made it part of me.

Even looking back at my circuitous route, the dots do somehow connect between the trailer park, all those apartments, and PennHenge. I've lived in unconventional homes and have been well-suited to them since I was a kid. I liked the social component of living with friends and didn't want to give that up just to find the stability of having my own home. I like self-reliance; I feel at ease counting on myself to get things done. Financially, I never signed on for more than I could handle, a lesson that came directly from my parents and was instilled from birth. I always pushed for cheap and livable rather than pricey and posh. I know I can't actually afford my own taste, so I don't even try.

In structure and in spirit, though, PennHenge could not be more different from the house my parents live in. That is partially by my design and partially subconscious, an effect of my yearning for a less restricted life. In over a decade of my owning and living in this house, my parents have never visited. Not one time. They live forty minutes away.

When I talk about the house with them, I have no idea what they picture. They must have Google street-viewed it, checked the particulars on the real estate sites, but other than that they have no basis upon which to visualize my stories.

When I bought the house, I knew they were worried about me. Though they kept their displeasure well contained, it was clear they thought I paid too much, that the level of upkeep would be insurmountable and the neighborhood threatening. At the beginning, I asked them to visit, but told them I needed some time to settle in first. When I brought it up again, maybe six months later, they seemed to have gone cold on it. They hated Providence—as they hate any and all cities—and didn't seem to be in a hurry to drive "all the way" here. I was flustered, and felt mildly rejected, but I was also quietly relieved by their apathetic reaction. If they never visited, I would never have to explain why this stair tread was loose or why that screen was ripped. I wouldn't have to cop to being the dawdling and imperfect homeowner that I am. Their home is so tidy, so stable. Nothing is in disrepair. I didn't think I was capable of unapologetically presenting them with my messy reality and just letting them call it as they saw it. I felt a need to protect them from knowing just how much of a heap PennHenge was; the other side of that coin was a comfortable insulation from their judgment. This place would never be a model of efficiency, cleanliness, or economy. I couldn't take what I was pretty sure would be their unintentionally obvious hatred of my new home, because it might feel like an indictment of the life I had chosen.

They didn't come over that year, or the next, and we slid into a groove of just not talking about a visit as an earthly possibility. I've always told them the tales of PennHenge, though I usually offer up an ever-so-slightly shinier and less weed-laden version than the real one. They know about my struggles and my successes. They know about my tenants and their relative oddities. They await the strawberries from my garden every year, and they give me gifts for the house. They've watched me fashion a pretty happy life from this initially questionable base of operations; they've watched me grow less anxious and more capable as a result.

I love my tiny family and want them to know the truth of my life. I want to stand up in front of them and say, "This is not what you would choose, but it's my constancy. This is not what you would choose, but it's mine and I have to love it and I actually do love it." And I would not apologize for the things that are dirty or broken or improperly aligned—either within the house or within myself—but instead I would say, "Come take a look. I think I've finally settled in."

Flip of Fools

I know something is wrong, deep down, before I do anything to actualize the thought. The usual springtime rhythms of our little side-by-side plots aren't picking up the way I've grown accustomed to. Normally at this time of year, mid-April, Angelo and Fiorella and I are on either side of our splintered wooden fence, readying our gardens for the growing season. We pick and snip last season's roots from the dirt, dried as they are from months of snow cover and cold. We break off hardened stalks from the perennials scattered throughout our beds, prepping for the pliable buds that are beginning to part the soil. We patch our hoses and scatter our compost. I've been intermittently at work in this manner for a couple of weeks, when it's warm enough, relishing the sun and the birdsong. I haven't seen Angelo or Fiorella, and I feel myself reflexively glancing at their house every few minutes. It looks shut down, still in winter mode. Their aging Ford is in the driveway. Over several days my concern intensifies, until I'm looking up at every sound, hoping to hear their banter, hoping to see them loping around, their goofy, yipping dog close behind.

One gray afternoon I finally see Fiorella. She's leaning over the porch railing, looking out toward the street.

"Fiorella," I call out. As she turns to me, my worry bubbles to the surface as I blurt, "Is everything okay?"

She looks at the ground. "Angelo died."

I guess I knew it already.

I hurry over to hug her and cry with her and to offer help. She's dressed in black. Her eyes are dull. She seems to barely recognize me. Her English is limited, and I have three phrases in Italian, none of them useful in this situation—but we speak a little, we get as far as we need to. "He very sick and it get worse a little, a little, a little," she told me. He'd been a heavy smoker for decades. I'd seen him carted off in an ambulance a couple of times. He often told me about his visits to the doctor and the medications he was on, always ending the conversation with a wave of dismissal and an "eh, what you gonna do?"

Our brief interaction seems to have drained Fiorella. With another hug and a promise to stop in soon, I retreat to my apartment. The street looks different.

How to quantify Angelo's legacy? He didn't need much. He reveled in his privacy and stayed close to home. He never made money—didn't seem to care for it. He didn't travel further than across town, at least in his older years; as long as I'd known him, I rarely spied him leaving the little compound he shared with Fiorella. In those days just after his death, I decide not to try to think him through. Instead,

I dedicate my garden that summer to his memory. I decide that every time I get tired of pulling weeds or stringing up trellises, I'll keep going a little longer, with him in mind. When I'm out there pulling garlic out of the ground, a breeze flipping the brim of my floppy hat, I'll meditate on him. He wasn't sentimental about his garden the way I am—he tended it solely for food, not to indulge some mystical longing of the soul—but I think he would forgive my maudlin tribute. He was not a meddler.

Over the following weeks, Fiorella lets me into her life, her home. I drop in to see her, bring her food, and help her decipher the mail. I make phone calls on her behalf. In the midst of one call to clear up some business with the government, I find out that she is eighty-four years old and that he was seventy-four, a rare age difference for an old country marriage of the early 1960s. I'd love to learn more about this one tantalizing detail, someday, but I can't imagine her talking about it. Some widows find comfort in journeying back to the beginnings of their long marriages; others would rather have a visitor stick to practical matters—the bills, car repairs.

Her apartment is comfortable, full of stuff but neat enough. She shows me where she banged her knee and the enormous dark bruise that resulted. She shows me the place where a pipe burst on the second floor last winter; the ceiling in her bathroom had to be taken down due to water damage and had never been fixed. She'd fallen on her way out of church, she said, but it was no big deal. Her roof leaked badly. Her car didn't always start. "I no have money," she said. I go home after these visits wondering how long she can stay in the house on her own, while at the same time registering her formidable strength. She is in pain, but she keeps moving. She isn't intimidated by the sudden realities of her life without Angelo. She works capably, knows her limits, knows where to go for support. She asks for help from her church community. Soon there are guys patching her house's chimney and siding and fixing the weak spots in her roof. A couple of her fellow parishioners bring groceries.

Eventually she catches up on her plantings, putting seedlings in the ground just in time for the season—and then quickly schooling me by producing a glorious variety of meaty tomatoes in large volumes.

I've guessed that some of Fiorella's helpers have inquired about whether she plans to move out of her house now that Angelo is gone. I thought about asking her that question myself, in those early days after her husband's death. The house is so much to handle. I decided to simply observe her and let her know that she can call me any time she needs help. I imagined a need to keep her safe, to find her an assisted living setting where she could live among many other people, to make sure she isn't alone. In Fiorella's situation, though, some people chuck safety and sterility in favor of the home and life they've spent their years building. A guarantee of supervision doesn't compare.

I'd love to talk with Fiorella about the neighborhood; she's part of a dwindling few who know from daily experience how much has changed in the last fifty years on Penn Street. I'd planned to talk more with Angelo about it, too, though it always amounted to an uncomfortable conversation. They stuck around when many of their Italian neighbors left— but why? Was it a choice? Were they constrained by finances? Did they love it here, or were they just stubborn? Do they have other family here? Kids? But whenever I engaged them even slightly in this line of questioning, Angelo and Fiorella offered one or two small nibbles and then shut me down. Perhaps there is something painful in their past that they didn't talk about. Or maybe they don't have the energy to find the words for it, to translate it for a different language and a different time. The secrets of Federal Hill are locked up tight. I'm ambivalent about the overworked stories of mob bosses and their henchmen; I want to know how ordinary people got by in those days.

Is there a comfortable place between the old Federal Hill of intimacy and calm criminality and the new Federal Hill, which is—like so many neighborhoods ravaged by the Great Recession—hurriedly turning its pockets inside out looking for money? A familiar frenzy is cranking up. A small two-family house around the corner from PennHenge went on the market on a Saturday and was sold by Monday. It's beautiful from the outside, but heavy with wood paneling and grim carpeting on the inside: a flip in the making? These hyperactive sales now dot the map; then the contractors' vans start pulling up, the sounds of sanding equipment and nail guns permeate. When I talk with others who own houses on nearby streets, the question is always the same: "Who *are* these people?" Who, indeed, are the people buying in, chasing an iffy gravy train in Providence, a city that makes tentative gains every decade or so, only to find itself unable to sustain them?

`Also: aren't we, along with the rest of the country, supposed to be in housing rehab right now? We did have that pretty bad crisis about a decade ago, and that kind of felt like a rock-bottom moment, but here we are again, so soon. Americans are so enamored of housing as a way to get rich and look rich, though, that we cannot stay away. Those new rules we made after the last crash? We can push 'em a little; we're *smarter* now. No way are we going to make those same mistakes again.

I wonder what Angelo would think of the old Italian social club on Courtland Street, less than a block from our houses, which was vacant for many years but is now being renovated, soon to reopen as the Courtland Club, according to its website (as of early 2017), a "meeting place for artists, tradespeople, thinkers, small business owners, and their guests and benefactors to gather, discuss ideas, and birth collaborations."

Putting aside that creepy jargon, the concept is not terrible. The ethnic and gender rules of the traditional social club were exclusionary by design. If we're going to resurrect social clubs, the model should be freed from those biases. On the face of it, a community idea-generating space sounds cool, even if it's just a glorified bar where self-defined "thinkers" are encouraged to gather. But there are still rules of exclusivity at work here: being a private club, applications can be rejected for any reason; if one is allowed to join, there is an annual membership fee of one hundred dollars. That doesn't sound like a lot of money, but many in the neighborhood don't have discretionary income. The club's original website mission statement makes it sound like a kind of philanthropic endeavor: "We are dedicated to the responsible and inclusive improvement of this neighborhood and the city of Providence." But this is a restaurant and bar—a business—and this business, I presume, will want to make money. Perhaps it will also turn out to be a shining example of inclusiveness and a champion of the average Federal Hill dweller, and I hope it does, but its message has a pretty bad case of tone deafness.* I understand that the proprietor believes that the club will be improving this little area in the heart of the Hill, but installing a neighborhood amenity that the neighbors themselves must pay to set foot in—an amenity that will naturally cater to more influential people driving in from tonier areas of town—seems duplicitous. Talk of improvement feels like a ruse, and anyway, people have varying definitions of that word. Months after construction on the club was underway, the owner began buying and renovating several of the multi- and single-family homes that surround the club, which when complete will likely result in

*A later iteration of the website dropped the rhetoric about benefactors and neighborhood improvement, instead touting the renovation's "contemporary and inclusive mindfulness."

higher rents and prettier facades to round out his personal village.

It is into this uncomfortably cold sea of economic lows and highs that Federal Hill is now thrown. A tide of unforgiving money is rising. Once a place finds a certain level of desirability, money works as an automaton to flood every space with its own unstoppable motion. It happens here not in the wildfire-like way it spreads in big cities, but nonetheless it's impossible to ignore. Rundown houses are gutted and modernized, made squeaky clean. Corporate entities grab foreclosures. Rents creep up; people are displaced. Buying a house or finding a stable long-term apartment in the neighborhood floats further out of reach for most of the people who want to live here.

Well-meaning acquaintances helpfully counsel me, a twinkle in their eyes, that the west side of Providence is a real estate "hot spot" right now. Guys drive around in pickup trucks pointing at houses, prospecting, taking pictures; amateurs and experts buy battered houses, fix up the apartments, flip them. When I get irritated by their entitled presence, I remind myself that I did the same thing. I came floating in, a newbie if ever there was one, when the housing market was way up; without educating myself I bought a house that was more than I could manage. I have only hoped to atone by sticking around, neither selling nor buying again, and I've outlasted my original expectations by doing just that.

It's a strange thing to live in somebody's hot spot.

I feel a little like a neighborly display, a not-psyched representative, as potential investors look at a house on the block. I don't wave; I don't smile or speak. I would prefer to disregard them entirely, along with the swings of the economic pendulum that brought them here.

Choosing a neighborhood is a political statement; so is staying in one. At twenty-seven, I thought my neighbors and I were on the same socioeconomic footing just because we lived on the same streets. I used to spend time shutting out my surroundings; I expended mental energy blotting out the noise and commotion, annoyed at people rather than choosing to try to know them. Many years ago, I called a perhaps twelve-year-old kid a "piece of shit" for dropping candy wrappers in front of my house as he walked down the street. In this unkind moment— even as the words were leaving my mouth—I knew I was entering dangerous territory. I was not seeing this kid's humanity; instead I was allowing his minor infraction to taint his very existence in my eyes. In general, too, I was letting the small irritants of my environment poison my connection to the people of the neighborhood, and I felt the wrongness of it. I had to stop there, to study and reject my insolence.

I—the white, college-educated, continuously employed lady whose still-married parents constantly opined about the value of a dollar—have unfathomable advantages over many of the people living around me. My privilege contributed to making me an owner here and not a renter. That I ever glossed over that fact isn't an easy admission. But having been here well over a decade, seeing the advances and the setbacks, the calm and the crazy, I know I'm now a better neighbor. I watch out for my neighbors; they do the same for me.

This is no manicured cul-de-sac. There is no veneer of faultlessness in Federal Hill; we neighbors do not pretend perfection. Nonetheless, the place has its beauties and its lessons.

With Federal Hill's lurid past subdued to a whisper, and a varied rush of people filling the vacuum left by the Italian American exodus, the neighborhood has no representative face. It certainly isn't one that looks like Angelo's. He never seemed bitter about that—about being the only Italian guy left on the block—but he was angry about people breaking into his car and hiding from the cops in his yard. He took a lot of pride in his modest home—I think because he felt that owning it was what truly made him part of his adoptive country. There's a faded, peeling "Proud to Be an American" sticker on his front door; I take this to be an immigrant's statement of solidarity with his chosen home. It's a pure and moving declaration in Angelo's hands, whereas in some bloviating Trump-lover's hands it reads like a boast of national supremacy. Every household in the Hill used to celebrate the same days, worship the same God, employ the same rhythms to mark their routines: Catholic mass, big Sunday meals, factory jobs, festivals, Dean Martin albums. I know Angelo missed this sense of unity (which some would call homogeneity). He believed that Federal Hill should be more conservative, stick to the classic edicts of church and family. Simple living. He didn't like the noise or the parties (some of which regrettably took place right next door at my house), and resented feeling that his home was at risk. When he caught young men in his yard or near his car, he told me, "I just say to 'em: *fuck you!*" It was the only time I ever heard Angelo swear in English.

Angelo was my anchor to the old neighborhood; I understood it in some measure only because I could look at him, hear him speak. With his death, I had some kind of internal proof that the old institutions of this place were ending. I was despondent for Angelo and doubly for Fiorella—two beloved individuals—but I finally felt sure that I would do best to leave behind the conflicted customs of Federal Hill's past, rather than pining for them as if they held some ethereal romance.

Record Odds

My most recent dip into singlehood has brought on a crisis of self that has me oscillating between loud, psyched-to-be-single, fuck-all-y'all bluster and weak, aimless, what-have-I-done-with-my-life blubber. It's tiring and pathetic. I sense that I look haunted, like my own life just exploded in my face. I've used up a lifetime of goodwill with my friends, who listen to my endless complaints and justifications and help me deconstruct the breakup again and again.

I work from home now; with no office to go to, I'm a singular outlier in the publishing industry and that's only intensified the isolation. I pity the co-worker who calls me with a simple question, because I am a talker, and I will *keep* that conversation going until it no longer serves a purpose.

I've started doing a fair amount of yoga to give myself a break from an irritating *what do I do now?* thought cycle. It works; while I'm in class I stop thinking, let myself be light and powerful, let my mind be an empty room with an open door. Later, of course, the room floods again, with all the junky questions I ask myself about dating and love and the future: How can there be anyone dateable out there whose variables align with mine? A single person nearing forty who is not gunning toward having kids, who finds me funny, likes my brain, and can handle my all-or-nothing dating style? Whose humor, intellect, and face I can admire? Whose plans for the immediate future might somehow fit with mine?

Being at home all the time is stifling, so I go out. As raw and on the surface as my emotions have been, people piss me off, but I seek them out anyway. Happy couples are problematic. Men are revolting, a bunch of self-absorbed babies who seem to think I should be competing for their interest.

I know it's unhealthy and futile, but I fret about getting old. I think of Seth, still in his twenties and living free, and feel jealous, like he sponged up the best I offered and left me to stagger, purposeless, into my forties. But whatever it was I offered, I did so freely, maybe blindly. Now my job is to extricate myself from the circle of regret I'm treading.

I picture a possible alternative to this consternation: Someday, when PennHenge and I go our separate ways, I'll buy a tiny bungalow not too far from the beach or on some alpine lake and hide out there for another twenty years. I'll hang up my landlady uniform and go off to this new place, luxuriantly stretch out on a lawn chair in the yard. I'll do yoga on the porch. I'll run trails with my dog. I'll garden like a maniac. I'll happily ignore the latest technology. I'll travel. I'll ride a rusty bike around my neighborhood and be that nice lady who lives alone and says "Hi" to everyone, even though no one says "Hi" anymore.

I can see tho house on its pad of green grass rolling

out in front of me, and it looks wonderful. I climb the stairs and step onto the porch, knock on a window, shade my eyes to look inside. It's sparse but warm, colorful, dotted with art. Flowers. Patterns. Plants. The older me is in there, writing, reading, or taking my time while cooking something labor intensive, just out of sight. I imagine those quiet, unscheduled days stacked up and waiting. Having time to linger in my own existence, relaxed into the aloneness.

But what about babies? The thought cycle cuts back in, scraps the self-affirming visualization. *Do I want to have babies? Now or never, dude.*

No, I tell myself, *I've always said I probably wouldn't, right? Why am I second-guessing this now?*

Well, obviously, it's because I've recently been dumped. I'm wondering if I blew my chance, if I'll die alone, you know, the most basic nagging questions.

When my thoughts become unguarded, the coiled snake of my brain lunges out to order me back to self-interrogating.

I have no answers with which to placate this inner dialogue, so I turn down its volume by drinking Vinho Verde with Dan and Steve, meditating, reading, and listening to music. In order to avoid penning email confessionals to Seth, Dan suggests that I rearrange my apartment and buy some furniture. I swap my office and bedroom; sleeping in a new room feels good. I cook myself nice food and spare no effort in doing so. I decide to resurrect my dusty stereo and buy some life-affirming music. My turntable needs a new needle, so one chilly, sunny afternoon, the old cartridge in my pocket, I take the five-minute walk to the nearest record store. The owner, Dave, is standing on the sidewalk in conversation with someone, a fact I overlook as I yell out, "Hey! *There's* the guy I'm looking for!"

If my mom were to concoct a pickup line, this is what she would come up with.

But I wasn't trying to throw come-ons at him. I really was just trying to get a new needle and shake off my solitude for five minutes. It was the end of winter, and most days I barely verbalized at all. I was forgetting how to speak to people without jumping all over them, pent up like a crated puppy. We talked for a few minutes. Dave guided my buying decisions; he tried to give me a discount; I refused it. I knew he and his ex had broken up around the same time that Seth and I had split, and he knew it too, so we were kind to each other, but kept it light.

Shortly after that interaction, a common Providence thing started to happen. Dave and I ran into each other more in a few weeks than we had in five years. Being single again, we were both going out, pretending everything was cool, socializing, but it was more than that. In a small city like Providence—one with a teeming music and art scene—you can think of someone you'd like to see, go to a public place, and conjure *him* up. You can make *her* choose to do the very thing you're doing that night; compel *them* to stop into that particular bar on that particular night. Part of it is a pleasantly proportional relationship between the number of appealing things to do on a given evening and the high number of like-minded people up for attending said events.

The rest is just Providence, something subliminal, some kind of kismet that can't be quantified other than in our dreams. Providence lifers attest to having dreams in which the city where we live becomes an amusement park, a futuristic utopia, or an enclave in the clouds. "It was Providence, but it wasn't *Providence,*" we say. The dream cast includes our friends, our exes, our mentors, our enemies, and they wave and smile beatifically, all debts and slights forgiven.

Out in the real city, the one with many faults and many magnificent people, Dave seems to be everywhere. I like the crinkly, smiley corners of his eyes; I like his voice. He's funny, charismatic, excitable, and full of life. Thoughtful. Game for the joyful wasting of time. Someone who will always take the conversation to an unforeseen place.

We're pleasantly keyed in, a good conversational fit. It's fun to realize I get along well with this person, especially after having seen him around town for years. Still, I barely know him, and although he is intriguing, I'm hanging back. No phone numbers are exchanged, no feverish texting or Snapchatting commences. It goes on like this for a while.

On one of my run-ins with Dave, we get into a discussion of our local minor league baseball stadium, a slightly dumpy old concrete fortress where the crowd is scrappy and fun, and the experience campy. We make lax plans to "maybe" see a game "sometime soon," but there is a stunning lack of urgency on both sides. A month later, we finally exchange phone numbers and make a plan to go.

Even with the long wait, I'm not prepared for it.

It happens to be Star Wars Night at the ballpark, which means a rare sold-out crowd and roving bands of overstimulated children dressed as Han Solo. Dave has a disposition to match: he heckles the players, he loudly claps, cheers, sings, and complains about the lethargy of the fans seated in our section; he has all of the kids in the vicinity laughing and anticipating his next joke. *Bit of a handful, this dude,* I think, while also smiling nakedly into his face. After the game, we go dancing, and then I drop him off at home, where we talk for another couple of hours. I go home thinking, *well, that might have been a thing?*

The next few times we talk on the phone, in the late evening as he prepares himself a negroni and goes out to his fire escape to watch the moon, it comes up that we've lived most of our adult lives within a mile of one another. We've been in the same room countless times, at parties, at shows, at bars, going back to the nineties when he arrived in Providence as a college freshman. I'd seen his bands perform. We track ourselves to this show, that festival, and find that the underpinnings of our lives line up along the same curve.

When you start talking along those lines, things can proceed in one direction only. Having presented ourselves to one another as simultaneously familiar and new, we drift into a carefree summer of beach trips and hikes. It smacks of a revisitation of youth, a nostalgic trip with our former selves, and we claim it without shame.

That year, for the first time in my life that I can recall, it rains heavily, all day, on the Fourth of July.

The neighborhood fireworks displays are silenced, shown up by thunder and massive, ripping lightning. Plans are cancelled; grills lay dormant. Dave and I happily spend the day in bed, freed from obligation. As we settle into probably our third nap, we hear another slash of lightning and a very loud and unclassifiable sound. I run to the window and see that a huge bough has torn from the tree just outside and is sprawled on the street. "Holy shit," I say, yawning, as I return to bed.

Dave lives in a mill building in an old industrial neighborhood once dominated by working factories. It's a cozy, open space with giant windows off of which he and his roommates have built their own rooms with sleeping lofts. Everyone takes care of the space; they keep it clean, cook together, and do small repairs. It's a communal living situation that actually works. Dave has filled his corner of "the mill" with records—shelf after shelf of meticulously maintained, carefully arranged records. This is his personal collection—the gems—and it is never to mix with the stuff for sale at the shop. While the records are kept in museum-ready condition, the rest of his room is not subject to such order. Stereo equipment is piled to the ceiling—most of it awaiting one crucial piece before it can be used. His bed is a twin mattress on the floor upstairs; there are a couple of metal poles strung up, between which his clothes are slung. There are a few other bits of furniture, all utilitarian objects in found condition. Books about music, baseball, and philosophy.

His priorities are clear, and I like where they are.

The store, of course, is another record reposito-ry. There are the front room records—the stuff for sale—and a slew in storage in the back. There is a hierarchy to the storage and filing system, but it's not terribly transparent unless you've happened to trip and fall into Dave's brain. I loved going into the store before I knew Dave, and part of what I loved, without knowing it, was his essence incarnate—his down-to-nerd-out, lovable goofball personality— posted up in every corner of the place. The people who worked there were charming and lively and without pretentiousness. The store was home to a range of music I found inspiring and overwhelming, and I'd often go in determined, flip through the stacks, and come out a half hour later, flustered, with a random calypso record—or some other thing I wasn't sure I wanted—in my hand.

Dave starts bringing records to my house instead of to the mill. We listen to old stuff, new stuff, and we decide which to keep and which should go back into rotation at the store. When I wax poetic about a record that had once been special to me, it is in my hands the next day, wrapped in brown paper, Dave's handwritten note stuck to it. I lower the needle onto the record, and we lie down on the rug, side by side, in front of the speakers, to get a good listen.

We are building something sturdy. Upon this frame, variables are aligning.

Thrillingly Optimistic

After a year of chance cohabitation, Dave moves into PennHenge. He's been living at the mill for the better part of ten years, so this must be bittersweet for him, but I can't find an ounce of conflict in his disposition. We clean out his space at the mill, and he rents a storage unit for the vastness of his record overflow. It quickly becomes piled to the rafters. Then Dave begins the process of further classifying the treasured records that made it into the house. The records for everyday listening—the ones that we want to hear again and again—end up in the living room alongside the stereo and a set of boss speakers that are overkill for a third-floor apartment. The records not likely to find themselves on heavy rotation—no less coveted, just less frequently spun—end up outside the door on the third-floor landing. There are more in the basement. A dehumidifier hums next to the boxes; climate control is crucial.

"I don't know, do you like this original Japanese copy of *Rumours*? I feel like the first American pressing is better. Boomier, earthier, definitely louder, you know?"

I can't always hear the difference, but I like being asked.

My books, his records: PennHenge now needs constant vigilance to keep it from creeping into hoarder territory. I'm not precious about my books—they're folded, creased, softened by my heavy-handed study. And I often give the extras away. I believe that's how they're best appreciated. But records—bought and sold on their condition—are sensitive, worth more money, susceptible to horrors brought on by heat, cold, dust, mold, overzealous handling, and haphazard storage. I cringe every time Dave takes one of my old records out of its sleeve because as a teenager I was a danger to keeping things nice, a maven of both overzealous handling and haphazard storage. "This one would be worth a hundred bucks if it wasn't so beat," he might tell me, quickly adding, "but it looks like you enjoyed it, so that's great."

I struggle with putting a new man in an old house, sometimes, especially when all the flotsam of my past seems to drift around us as we perch up here on the third floor. The physical space hasn't changed much since James lived here with me. I dream, once, that Dave is speaking to me the way James sometimes did, toward the end: "Why don't you clean the fuckin' litter box? It stinks!" I yell back at him: "I cleaned it *last night!*" When I wake up, after a moment of ill reminiscing, I feel an acute sense of peace, a pleasant heaviness that illustrates how much my inner landscape has changed.

As "the landlady's new boyfriend," Dave could be a real nuisance to my tenants, but he is golden, the perfect buffer. He manages to be vocal without throwing his weight around. He is a master of wielding humor to solve problems. He's a grounding force.

Testing the waters of working together, Dave and I take on a few projects. We clean out a particularly junk-filled room in the apartment, paint it, seal the floor and buy some midcentury furniture from Craigslist. We get rid of stuff, then organize what's left. We have yardwork days; we cut down invasive trees and vines and trim back the plants that have gone out of shape. We both find this work highly meditative. There are smaller things, too—the unclogging of drains, the fixing of toilets, the turning of compost. We alternate between wordless concentration and the briskly paced cracking of jokes, interspersed with frequent kissing. It's not the quickest way to get a job done, but you can't squabble about petty shit when you're kissing.

I never feel embarrassed around this person; so often in the world I feel like I've said the wrong thing, or said too much, but never to Dave. He takes me at my most irritable, dorky, tentative, or premenstrual, and he encourages those expressions. Having that kind of freedom and emotional rigor in a relationship allows for far-and-wide explorations of one's inner workings. My old tendency toward romantic speculation, of striving to figure a person out and then trying to force our goals to coincide, has abated. There is no wondering when things will change, when the circumstances will be right.

Is this where I tell you that we got married?

I certainly can't leave that fact for the very end,

as if it's the payoff to this lonesome story of a lady and her house, struggling together, biding our time, waiting for a sweet and caring man to come along and make this drafty old shithole a home.

That isn't how it went, but man, I am glad he came along.

Despite the risk of suddenly sending this story marching up to the summit of Mount Platitude, I have to tell you that we got married; it was beautiful, and we are colossal together.

He hasn't made over the house in grand style or fixed all of its problems. He's not a jacked furniture maker, or a tough-guy builder, or a sleek rich dude (as if), or any romantic male/domestic fantasy archetype, besides being a willing taker-out of garbage. So we are safe from perfection. The house is still a mess, but we're happy.

After two years together, a couple of months before my fortieth birthday, we start kicking it around. There's no ring, there's no dramatic proposal; in our excitement, we just make the decision together. We start making plans for Maine in mid-September, which is two-and-a-half months away.

A week or two after the decision is thrillingly official, with our parents informed and plans just underway, we spend the Fourth of July in rural Vermont with Dave's old buddy/bandmate and her family, and a crop of friends. The night before, we arrive and set up our tent in a clearing overlooking rolling hills, a few friends' tents surrounding our own. The sweet little crowd assembled there are among the first people we inform of the upcoming wedding;

a cheer goes up into the dusk. On the Fourth, we ready for a party, and an impromptu stage is set for the bands playing that day. People arrive and lay out their blankets, the music begins, and I let a child paint my face like a butterfly, the antennae curling up my forehead. It's easy to fantasize from this perfect, revelatory place that the ugliness in the world has disappeared, that it isn't crazy to be optimistic, to be taking romantic leaps in this time of national and global turmoil. Then some bad campfire music breaks our reverie, and Dave and I retreat to our tent, where we laugh and goof around like two nearly forty-year-old kids.

A month later, in August, I do actually turn forty. Going against all that a younger me had ever heard or believed about that threshold, when the day comes I am excited to cross it. Lying in the sand on a deserted beach at the tip of a little island, shutting my eyes against the gleam of high Rhode Island summer, I feel young, strong, ferocious with life force. In late bloomerism there is much to embrace.

Having observed unhappy "older" women all my life, I'd assumed I too would be miserable by now. Reaching adulthood wasn't what I thought it would be, didn't have to be the way I saw it internalized by some women I'd known—as a constantly building litany of trying tasks and overstated dramas to be endured from under the thinnest veil of acquiescence. A well of unreleased rage and knowing confinement seethes just under that veil. Our culture makes it this way, of course; we don't choose it. Endless stipulations are imposed on us before we're born. But in gaining a single degree of separation from cultural expectations, a space flares open. A little at a time, we push back and find there is room to divine our own spirit.

The plumber is named Matteo. He comes on a Sunday morning in September; it happens to be the Sunday before the wedding, and three days before Dave and I are to leave for Maine, where the wedding will be held. The house, sensing my imminent departure, sensing my dangerous level of happiness and that my energies are focused elsewhere, has asserted its power over me one last time in my waning single life, as usual in the form of water where it shouldn't be.

By the time he enters the house, Matteo and I have already had a driveway-based conversation about how sad he is to see the state of his old neighborhood. He says he was born on my street—a few houses down—and has lived in Canada, and in Italy, and now he's back in Rhode Island. "It's a long story," he says.

He speaks softly. His downturned face displays a look of pity for me.

"It's really not bad, I mean, it's not exactly paradise, but I like it! I've been here a long time," I say, with overenthusiasm, really just to clamp this conversation shut. His sympathy, besides being totally unwarranted, is delaying an investigation of the pipes. I try to steer the conversation back to mechanical matters, as he is a plumber and not a leisurely gentleman caller just visiting for the hell of it. He joins the long line of sad-faced repairmen who seem to wish they could protect my small, white woman's body from the horrors of this bad place and these bad people who are all around me, these obviously terrible, shadowy characters—who in truth haven't so much as uttered an unpleasant word in my direction in twelve years and counting.

Dave comes home while Matteo is working on fixing the problem, and true to form, immediately engages him in a conversation about politics, religion, Trump, all the hits. At first, it is amusing to listen to Dave make a case for his humanist beliefs with an argumentative plumber, but the tenor of the interaction goes sour when Matteo—casually fingering a wrench—spouts off a couple of racist proclamations. We do our best to argue that his attitude is all wrong. Eventually we have to awkwardly shut down the conversation just so that the job at hand can go on and this man can leave our home.

After fixing the main problem at long last, Matteo tells me there is bad news: when a tenant shut off the flow of water to his apartment to avoid flooding, he must have loosened some sediment in the pipes, for there is now a blockage in the plumbing somewhere between the first and second floors. The second and third floors now have no water. He provides Dave and me with a few tips as to how we might find the clog, although he admits these usually don't work. If we can't locate and clear it, he says, we'll need to cut into the first-floor ceiling and replace all of the pipes in that part of the house so that water will flow freely again. He'll get the plumbing company in touch with us tomorrow morning to get the first appointment set up. Oh, and heads up, *it's going to be expensive.*

"We're . . . getting married in six days?" I sputter, as if that might grant us a reprieve.

"Aw, man, yeah, I'm sorry, that's tough. We'll get it fixed. Well, see you guys," he says, hoists his tool-box and is gone.

Dave and I begin our investigation, monkeying with every faucet in the house, unscrewing various pieces of plumbing, turning knobs, jiggling anything that can jiggle. Dave calls friends for advice. They too are stumped. We are worked into a lather, picturing the shitstorm that will commence when this repair job gets going, and the cartoonish bill we'll get: will it be five thousand dollars? Ten thousand? Not to mention that we have no water on two floors of the house and are soon leaving for a week to have a *super romantic no-stress wedding time!*

I'm palpitating in this manner when Dave says, "Let me just look around one more time." We head back to the basement; he searches for unturned stones. He flips a blue lever near the ceiling, and I hear the triumphant song of water rushing back into the pipes throughout the house. There was no blockage; there will be no tearing apart of any portion of the house; best of all, there will be no gigantic red-inked bill.

Flipping that lever should have been the first thing Matteo did after finishing the repair. *He's a plumber.* He knows this shit. He was too busy delivering his fearful screed to think straight. Dave and

I got so thrown off that we too almost missed the simplest solution imaginable. If we needed a practical reminder that fear and hate are eternally bad for the soul, bad for the mind, even bad for business, here it was.

Compulsively engaging with people is a tricky game—sometimes they test out their most despicable stuff from out of nowhere. I'm trying to get better at reacting thoughtfully, calmly, and firmly, especially when the person in question is being paid by me, yet tries to control me in my own home.

Having restored order, recounted Matteo's professional ineptitudes to the plumbing company, secured a partial refund, and escaped the awful world of pipes and drywall for a minute, Dave and I embark on a final, frantic stage of wedding prep. We assign bulky items like giant speakers, turntables, and coolers to friends to be brought to Maine. Thinking fondly of Angelo, I make jam from his precious grapes to give away as wedding favors; I gather a foothill-sized amount of vegetables from my friends' farm. Dave pulls an all-nighter making mixtapes of dinner music. We check with his parents, and mine, to make sure their cars are packed and any required items are on board. We pack our clothes and our hiking boots and our bathing suits. I wrangle all the stuff I'd been setting aside for weeks: dessert plates, silverware, tablecloths, candles, extension cords, the rings, the marriage license. We check with our officiant, the company renting us tables and chairs plus a lone porta-potty, and our friend who lives a few minutes from the wedding site. The guest list is tightly nailed down at forty people, but arranging food, drinks, and music for even that small a crowd is foreign to me.

It takes us five hours to pack the car, which has us antsy, mentally overheated. But as soon as we get on the highway, we start squealing. We've dodged doom in our domicile, we're en route to the coast of Maine, and we're going to ignore America's impending ruin—it's less than two months before the 2016 election—for an entire week because we're about to get wicked marital in one of the most relaxing places on earth, where the Wi-Fi is spotty and iPhones seem sort of ridiculous.

We arrive in Sedgwick, Maine very late at night and take a moonlit look around the place where we'll be fully nuptialized in a few days. The water in the nearby harbor twinkles under a just-shy-of-full moon; the grounds are leafy; the dense flora rustle with the sounds of nocturnal animals. The grass is thick and wet. The house—a stout, white, mildly creepy-looking home built in 1817—glimmers an inky blue under the night's light. We chose this location sight unseen, via FaceTime with the help of my friend Caitlin, a local, who came to tour it on a rainy day in July.

"Yeah, I think this is gonna work out," we yell to each other from various spots in the moonshadow. I can't see Dave, but I can hear his smile.

We unload the crucial stuff from the car and gingerly enter the house. We walk around turning on lights, checking out rooms; one of the lights turns itself off. We both see it happen. Dave and I verbally make note of it, but don't discuss it any further; meanwhile, he is sure of a spirit presence, and I'm leaning toward an electrical problem. My position on the matter is determined mainly by a need to stay calm, to not freak out. I would rather not fixate on the image of a haunted wedding, so I decide to ignore it as we settle in for the night.

As it went, if any spirit visited us, it was a detail-oriented one, and definitely female—a helpful apparition who fully grasped the length of our to-do list. Two days before the wedding, our parents and friends begin to arrive; wearing giant smiles and beaming forth love and calm, they set up tables and chairs, string up lights, pick flowers. By the time Saturday rolls up, I feel the expected stress, but I'm also floating around, grinning, confident that the crew will make sure everything gets done. "What a great group of friends you have," our parents all say independently of one another.

And then, in a flash, we are married. As my mom likes to note, very few bits of our ceremony are copied and pasted from elsewhere. "If you're looking for traditional, you've got the wrong girl," she says. "There was no 'Here Comes the Bride,' no 'Till death do us part,' no 'I do.' Made me nervous." Instead, a psych band—new friends from Maine whose music we'd connected with—play beautifully for the occasion, before and after the ceremony. Dave and I wear ornate masks made out of flowers and leaves, which we remove at the start of the ceremony in the spirit of coming to one another fully engaged and unguarded, having cast off our various preconceptions. I blubber uncouthly through the entirety of my vows. At the end of the ceremony, we ask the guests to circle up, hold hands, and chant with us: *"Let our light harmonize with the universe!"*

And we did beam our light that night—if not throughout the universe, at least around a sleepy town on the coast of Maine.

Closing the Circle

My family has always been three. Being the sole child of two people together for life is a pretty intense thing—you get the intimacy of being one-third of the whole deal, but you also get the intimacy of being one-third of the whole deal. You're a lynchpin of sorts, a barometer of the relationship and the focus of much parental energy. Dave's an only child too; when we learned that about one another, it became obvious why we get along so well. (We have dibs on the name Only Child for our forthcoming sappy/mystical space jam band.) Dave's parents married in 1969; mine in 1971. Both couples are still together, still doing most things in tandem.

Their marriages, though, were built in a different time than the one Dave and I have just embarked on. It is unfathomable to Dave and I that any relationship begun in one's twenties could hold up for fifty years, but they've done it. I know it was difficult for our parents to watch us both make some wayward love choices, starting up and then breaking up over and over, while they thought of that process as the dominion of teenagers, wondered when we would get over that already. But there is value in having one's heart trampled once or twice or fifty times. There is a degree of pleasure in flailing and being lovelorn at various moments in life.

Dave entered my life without hesitation, made his aims known. For the first time I was able to unabashedly let my parents observe the goodness of my relationship. Dave's positive energy, newly added to the family, forces fresh air between me and my parents. I knew I had never fully transformed my role from child to adult; where once I found that reassuring, as if nothing would change and no one would get old if I kept playing the part of the freckle-faced kid, I saw it now as holding us back. I'd long obscured the full truth of my life in hopes of avoiding difficult conversations, being judged, or causing worry.

Does it take only children a little longer to grow up? Maybe so. The cultural slogan is that we're selfish, sheltered, bad at empathy, introverted. That must be a conspiracy started by the multi-baby-family lobby, because in my travels it's not true. If there's a quality that I can say runs through every only child I know, to some degree, it's the tendency to be a late bloomer: to take a lot of time to figure out our place in the world. We don't have siblings to band with, who might prod us into having adult opinions or conversations as we get older. The family dynamic stays fairly static. We don't have an equal in the family, whether ally or enemy: all input is parental. Our households are generally quiet, meditative affairs, begetting careful, purposeful children. We have significant private time in which to ruminate, pick our way through the thorns of childhood existence, and come up with some real doozies that we believe until age and experience tells us otherwise.*

I'm twentysomething years past the point of getting by on innocence and my own nutball brand of logic, thank the goddess. I've staked out a good life. My parents seem to grasp that I am content to make decisions that fall a little outside the norm, and put no pressure on me to do anything differently. Without one critical piece, though, I know we can't move on from the pleasant but restrained communication style we've adopted.

They have to see PennHenge.

So I make the required overtures.

Dave and I are visiting my parents, perhaps a month after the wedding. We're in the post-dinner phase, all four of us occupying our own chair in their small living room in front of their enormous TV, a baseball game on mute. The conversation goes quiet for a minute, and then another minute, and I think, *Go for it, dude. It's never going to be easier than it is right now.* I should have warned Dave, but it's too late for that.

I employ a conversational tactic that helps me to

---

*Mortifying example: As a child, I believed that all babies had penises, which fell off at maybe three years of age, after which point everyone had a vagina. This thinking resulted from my careful consideration of my two younger male cousins' diaper changes. I'd never seen a naked baby, I guess, so I let them stand in for all of humanity's infants. I saw a really odd little appendage—I don't know whether I'd yet learned the word *penis*—and I stored the image away, vowing in this time of pre-internet bewilderment to figure it out later. My eventual conclusion was that I, too, once had the weird thing, but because I was no longer a baby, I'd lost mine, like a tooth.

broach challenging topics: I imagine I'm acting in a movie and these are my lines. I take myself out of it, just for the first couple of sentences, until I'm barreling through, reluctance forgotten.

Dave's face, eyebrows up, displays his intrigued surprise as I get started. My tongue trips once or twice, but I finally succeed in requesting their presence at a tour of PennHenge. Why did I wait so long? You'd think it's an invitation to Buckingham Palace the way I'm formalizing it. My mom is initially defensive, as if by mentioning the extraordinary amount of time that has passed without a visit (or even a mention of one) I'm accusing her of not caring. But I know that's not the case, and I tell her: the real culprit is something less concrete than that, something to do with keeping the peace, even at the expense of inhabiting our relationship in full. It takes some assurances, but they agree to the visit.

As the day of their arrival approaches, I hold myself back from cleaning every crevice of the house. It's my instinct to do just that—to scrub the place into respectability—but I want them to see our actual state of being. I need to be honest about the way we live. So I do the basics—make the bed, do the dishes, a quick lap with the vacuum cleaner—and I leave it at that.

Of course, the event itself is without incident, a molehill that I'd long since mountainized. They arrive ten minutes late due to directional challenges. I go out to meet them as they pull up out front; we saunter around the house while I rapid-fire talk them through. They check out the late-season garden and the legendary grapevines. After ten minutes, we go inside and they slowly climb the stairs to our third floor. They politely avoid comment on the cache of records that lives on the landing outside the apartment, though I can't resist commenting on them just to say they're "slowly but surely" going to the store to be sold. (It's true, sort of, but *Shut up already,* I think, *remember your mantra about them just seeing the place how it is.*) They do the barest inspection possible, not focusing 100 percent on any given area, clearly not wanting to pry or appear too critical. I run around showing them things, speaking maybe a little louder than is necessary. We don't run into any tenants; the street is quiet; the weed and cat poop bouquet in the hallway is mercifully subdued that day.

For all my fear and avoidance of this moment, they don't seem to judge. They are respectful; they ask questions, we laugh; all the stories they've heard gain concreteness. They don't go around peering into cupboards or checking for dust. They enjoy their fifteen-minute tour, and then we all go out for a nice lunch, because why not reward ourselves for defeating inertia and closing this gap? All through the meal, I'm giddy: the intention of the day is realized. They now know the physical reality of my life; they know not only whom I've chosen to live with, but where and what. The why may never be clear.

I doubt these two suburbanites will be hankering for weekly visits to PennHenge. But it doesn't matter: I know the limits of such things, and I'm proud of all of us. This isn't to be a bombshell dropped on our relationship; none of us is looking for radical change. But I hope it makes them see that I'm trying to bring them closer.

When it comes to the house, I still tend to speak of the future as "I" and not "we." I bought this place, I've kept the lights on and the roof 95 percent free from caving in for almost a decade and a half, and I alone own both the hardships and the benefits of this daft experiment. When Dave first moved in, I felt a defensive need to keep all of that to myself, to block him from paying bills, fixing stuff, and being tough with customer service reps on my behalf. I'd gotten used to it being *my thing*, no help needed, thanks. But now I have this excellent human being in my life who wants to help—and who should be free to help—because he is my partner, emotionally, legally, financially, in all things. He has a stake in PennHenge, and a say in its future, just as he is affording me with his business.

Governing this house is the only tangible power I've ever believed I had; as reluctant as I was to take that power at first, now I'm reluctant to give a little of it away. But I'm starting an alliance with Dave, sharing that power with someone who responds with reason and understanding. It is freeing; no crisis comes when he takes on new responsibilities! Other adults in the world are capable of good decision-making! I'm getting over myself!

Now that we're married, confronting a life spent at PennHenge and considering what that might require of us, it's time for a reckoning with this place.

At the least, we have to examine where we are, if we want to stay and/or could afford to leave. We think about this often, but the conversation is usually circular. Some days we're convinced that aging any further in this apartment might sap us of our good humor, our motivation. Then we step outside and have a great conversation with a neighbor, the birds singing in the trees above our heads, and leaving the neighborhood becomes unthinkable. Maybe we should be enacting a plan to start anew, but Penn-Henge is at its core a complicated home, and it's not letting us go easily.

Taking stock of my earthly property doesn't simplify the matter: Okay, let's see, we've got one trashed, darkened hovel that smells like stale pee and cigarettes (first floor); one fully restyled, millennial-friendly tech dome complete with multicolored iPhone-controlled LED lights and chandeliers (second floor); and one charming but outdated apartment heated by a single gas stove and painted in all the colors of a basket of Easter eggs (third floor). Plus a basement that looks like it has hosted several criminal enterprises. We're spanning several eras, and not gracefully. Who's going to buy this? These parts do not look at all like they belong to the same whole (or hole). For all my fixing and maintaining, I may only have made the place *less* desirable, unless I can find some freak like me to buy it.

Dave and I talk about renting out our third-floor apartment, moving down to the first floor, gutting that apartment, and bringing it back to basic livability as a long-term stopover on a distant journey to moving out of PennHenge. But that means we'd have to boot Elvin and Kenny (and Elvin's new ladyfriend, who has recently moved in with them). Elvin and Kenny haven't exactly treated the place with the utmost care over the years, but I don't relish the idea of laying this news on them, of giving them a deadline to GTFO after all this time. They are dug in; they'll never leave if I don't tell them they have to. But enacting such a deadline brings up other questions: I don't know if they could afford to get another apartment in the neighborhood, and as someone who complains about the gentrification and prettifying of these streets, that idea distresses me. What are my obligations to them after more than a decade? What are their obligations to me? There's no lease. Conversations are scarce. They slip their rent checks under my door in the middle of the night. It's amazing that we can live in the same little building and so rarely see one another.

Maybe they'd yell at me if I asked them to leave. Maybe they'd be sad. Or maybe they'd be relieved to end what they see as an obligation to me. Maybe they'd be happy to be forced to start fresh.

Had they kept the space about as nice as they'd found it—admittedly, even then, not *that* nice—I'd accept them staying on indefinitely. But their standards have slipped pretty far. I'm sure they no longer see the dirt and smell the nicotine, the same way I overlook the paint cans and stacks of books upstairs.

It's not like I've never tried to make rules—I have definitely laid down some kind of law regarding chain-smoking in the house; breaking stuff and silently hoping it will fix itself; turning the driveway into a junkyard; bad parking etiquette. But I've failed to adequately internalize that I have to repeat them over and over, even if I'm talking to the same old tenants I reminded last time. There's no institutional memory in this joint. The longer I do this job, the less enthused I am about reciting and repeating the policies of PennHenge. The guys on the first floor are slowly annihilating their apartment, while Colin, unchecked, creates his showplace, unearthing his drill and hammer every night just as Dave and I are settling in to watch Stephen Colbert on *The Late Show*.

When the day of the first-floor exodus does come, it's going to be supremely expensive to rip out the kitchen and bathroom, in some places down to the studs and the subfloor, rebuild it, and replace the sinks, toilet, tub, and appliances, but that and other costly repairs is what it needs. Another reason I've stalled out where I am.

I shiver at the thought of Dave and I living in that apartment. It's not just the dirt, the mold, and the garbage. Over the decade and change since the first floor has turned over, and especially since Caroline's departure, I've grown to feel like there's some bad juju tied up in there, and I don't want to be the one to rattle it loose. As if that wouldn't be trying enough for our fledgling marriage, the idea of living in a renovation environment of horrible daily discoveries does not appeal, either. I've been down this road before, and I know how these things go: "Well, we can't put in the toilet until we have the flooring down, and we can't put the flooring down until we have the tub plumbing in." Friends, I've gone through too much digestive distress not to have access to a working toilet. Just *no*.

So a sort of stasis has taken hold. Everyone on the first floor stays where they are, none of us particularly delighted with that fact; I would like things to change, but I haven't yet devised a realistic path for that change to take.

Instead of wallowing in the catch-22 that is the actual state of this all-too-real house, I soothe myself with a variety of dreamy thoughts of other houses. My fantasy house road forks in two directions: one goes to a simple, solid, small house either in the density of the city or out in the old, gray New England woods; the other goes to an off-the-grid, solar-powered homestead that is the antidote to the bloat of America's big, empty cardboard cul-de-sac monstrosities. The former is a fairly logical, sound next step if you think not terribly much will change over the next couple of decades; the latter is a total life modification that may sound insane and overreactive right now, but could put us in a pretty plum spot should our rocketing little planet encounter any extreme environmental turbulence.

I'd like to keep right on living the way I'm living now, in a "regular" house that draws on utilities and water from public sources. It's comfortable and known and it's how we've set up our neighborhoods, the setting from which we view our culture. I am truthfully not all that excited to learn the difference between gray water and black water. But the more I learn about climate change, the less sure I am that our current options are always going to be there for us. Especially considering the rate at which we're currently withdrawing from the Bank of Earth. Do not mistake me for a prepper or survivalist—I don't delight in the idea of outliving the rest of humanity in a darkened bunker, eating cans of beans and shooting anything that moves outside. I'm simply saying that it seems like a not-terrible idea to at least contemplate the radically changed world that might confront us in our lifetimes. We should all be learning how to grow at least a few types of vegetables, even if we're planting them in old buckets or coffee cans and placing them on our fire escapes.

There's a heating and air conditioning company with the motto, "Live in a World of Total Comfort." Such coddling bullshit; we live in an uncomfortable world! We should be learning *now* to live without luxuries like a constantly regulated seventy-degree interior environment, hamburgers, Cheetos, big, gas-devouring vehicles, leaving the lights and the giant TV on in an empty room, throwing everything "away." Instead we're sponging up as much of everything as we can, buying more on Amazon, somehow thinking it's patriotic to do so.

A couple of months before we got married, Dave and I watched a documentary about radically sustainable green buildings called earthships, and started fantasizing about the idea of running off to Taos to take up with the off-the-grid freaks. Earthships, built with earthen and recycled materials, include systems that provide thermal/solar heating and cooling, solar and wind electricity, self-contained sewage treatment, water harvest and re-use, and food production. Comfy in a desert setting, they're these curvy, colorful, one-of-a-kind, ultra-whimsical buildings that often look like a cross be-tween a mosque and something from the cover of a Yes album. They're practical yet dreamy, and possi-bly capable of holding back the effects of nightmare climate change.

Dave and I have also given a lot of thought to buy-ing or building an off-the-grid house in Vermont or Maine, or in Canada. Something insulated to within an inch of its life, with solar panels, battery packs, and a trusty wood stove. But we're staring down a very deep divide between our current reality and this possible new one. *Why not be adventurers?* we say, fully aware that we are not necessarily pos-sessed of a trailblazing spirit. We like the idea, but frankly, we have no clue how our everyday existence would look. We're not quite adventurous enough to log that point in the plus column. And then the con-versation veers: we both have jobs we love, and *oh yeah*, there is a record store and tens of thousands of vinyl slabs to consider. We're left with the frustrat-ing notion that these two worlds don't meet, or at least that we'd have to give up every physical thing we value to make the switch to sustainability. And then it begins to feel insurmountable. I'm not saying that the conversation ends there, just that we have a lot of reality checks to kick around.

Seeking some middle ground, I look into energy-conserving updates for the house and learn that blown-in and attic insulation alone would cost me five grand. With all my thoughts of environmental maximizing, PennHenge just looks even more like an inefficient beast, a relic of America's inflexible homebuilding tradition, which was and is based on untenable standards of uniformity and largesse. The cosmetic concerns often outweigh the practical ones, and the priorities for builders (and buyers) still ignore sustainable practices like situating buildings for the best use of sunlight or wind. Change is tough to come by when somebody already got here and fucked it all up, literally cast their mistakes in bricks and mortar. Those who do want to push things along have to tear down or build around what's already here.

This Must Be the Place

I'm not always in disaster mode, although I am often frustrated by our country's extreme lack of environmental leadership. I try to ignore the grim possibility that humanity may soon shrink away like a waning moon. Hoping to counteract our dismal moods and do something positive in reaction to election results and the general awfulness of our country's political outlook, at the end of 2016 Dave and I adopt a rescue dog, a black-and-tan Shiba Inu with a stoic face, an authoritative personality, and a little blocky body. She's our dream doggie. Her previous owners named her Foxy; we rename her Runi. She and I go for lengthy walks around the neighborhood in the winter. We usually take the side streets; the main thoroughfare in the neighborhood makes her anxious. As she pees on her forty-fifth snowbank, I get contemplative, thinking about how great she is, how much I love Providence, how shitty and how nice our neighborhoods are. We look into lovely spaces I never would have noticed had she not pooped on them.

One day, as we meander, I look up and see it: the house of my Providence dreams. It's a small, two-story single-family house of an unremarkable architectural type. Real estate reconnaissance later tells me it's 1,300 square feet and was built in 1850. It's been redone, now a monochrome dark gray with black shutters and a sweet slatted door painted . . . what is that? Chartreuse? It's only five or six blocks from PennHenge, on a street that looks like a slightly less beat-up version of my own: mostly tenements with a few older single-family homes sandwiched in. The house is so solid-looking, so tidy, so well-kept, and yet it seems to have a good sense of humor, like it's winking in my direction. I don't even *need* to see the inside, I recount to Dave breathlessly, because the outside is so beautifully done, I know it must be simple, tasteful, and warm, with a really organized kitchen and two cozy little bedrooms upstairs.

I love this house so hard, I'm surprised my smoldering eyeballs haven't set it on fire yet. This little confection embodies every guilty house fantasy I've had during my years of holing up on the third floor waiting for the walls to stop shaking. It's small and forthright, no tenants, no graffiti, simple, clean and linear: everything I wish for when PennHenge derails.

I can tell that whoever lives in this house isn't leaving anytime soon. This beauty is so lovingly restored, so well taken care of, no detail skipped over, that I've guessed this is someone's life project. Nonetheless, I've set up a "house alert" on some soul-crushing real estate app that will tell me immediately if the house goes up for sale.

One day I see a moving truck parked right in front of my house crush, and I'm dopily hopeful. My heart skips a beat, and my little dog and I practically run over to eavesdrop on the details. Her urinary needs provide a convenient cover as we stand just off to the side and loiter next to the truck. A guy comes out of the house across the street, toting a cardboard box. "Damn," I say to Runi, "it's not gonna happen, girl," as if she cares. She's perfectly happy at PennHenge, and why shouldn't Dave and I be, too? All of our needs are covered: food, water, warmth, love, music.

I'm exhausted by my human aspirations. We spend our lives working up to something, and when we finally get it, we start finding its faults. I'm never going to own that house, and if I did, I would find something therein to be unhappy about. So there is nothing to do but harness every bit of joy we can muster right here in our cramped apartment in our big, unruly house with our little dog. In our insane world. While we do that, we discuss the future and the feasibility of leaving here someday, but I refuse to let my ego do the buying next time, to mortgage my life just to get another mortgage. For now, we stick around and let our plans be fluid. We try not to feel as if we're waiting for something, because now is pretty good.

Our homes are wrapped up with our inconsistencies, our faults, our virtues, and our victories in one anarchic package. The mess is not always to be swept away, because we are in there somewhere.

In college, when I moved with my lady crew into our first apartment, I used to go for long walks by myself in all seasons. I'd shove a few bucks in my pocket for a coffee or a slice of pizza and set off to observe the goings on in Bristol, our small town on Narragansett Bay. I craned my neck to make note of swaying trees, birds on their swooping way to the water. Wood and brick buildings, gable roofs and storefronts, old schoolhouses, glowing white mansions with glossy lawns. I listened to the banter outside the diner or at the post office, the old Rhode Islanders getting their stamps, talking politics and weather. Portuguese, Yankee, Italian, English, Irish. Undertones of histories bumping up against one another; bending, blending, resigned to just being America. Blue collar and white collar. Fishermen and professors.

This town has a terrifically well-preserved collection of historic houses built in the 1700s and 1800s. Most are stunning buildings with regal features—peaks and cornices, columns and arches—all polished up in a manner befitting the showplace of the neighborhood. On those walks I often found myself slipping into a covetous reverie over the grand homes of Bristol. The same happened when I moved to Providence and began to pick my way around the opulent old houses of the East Side. I worshipped their good looks, their symmetry, their visual oddities, the unattainable wealth and rarity they signified. But like those of many beautiful old American places, the roots from which these houses sprung are hideously corrupted. It's an uncomfortable fact that a significant measure of both towns' early wealth was generated by the slave trade. The ports of Newport, Bristol, and Providence, Rhode Island, were extremely valuable stops within the triangular trade pattern between the slave markets of the African coast, the sugar-growing slave plantations of the Caribbean, and the rum-manufacturing ports of New England.

And we wonder why so many old houses around here are said to be haunted. The haunting need not be a literal spirit on patrol; perhaps it is just an unsettledness, a shiver. Our modern towns cannot help but remain tethered to these ghoulish days of the commodification and theft of human lives. I imagine that there is a heavy and eternal psychic toll on the places that harbored the people responsible for such acts, places that were active or complicit in America's early movement toward enshrining systematic white repression of black people and the other in all things.

Imagine each of these stately houses claimed by black families, rather than being passed around by white people to other white people for a million dollars a pop. Could be the sole cure for the haunting.

Our homes are not what we think they are. If we knew their secrets, we'd not find them so precious. History is inscribed therein; our history is glorious and hateful and squared upon the single-minded pursuit of money, and every grand old house testifies to it.

In avoidance of supporting New England's eerie patrician history, I now seek out the less distinctive, the less valued, the less traditionally adored houses. The ones that did (and continue to do) the tough work of sheltering regular people who sometimes didn't have the money to keep them pristinely preserved. The utilitarian places that encompass a quieter beauty and confess to the messiness of life.

PennHenge, I'm looking at you.

After all these years of upmarket dreams, am I back at your splintered, faded door, hat in hand, flowers behind my back?

Considering another home—which in a way amounts to considering another life—has always carried with it a sense of relief, as if PennHenge is a problem to be solved. There has been plenty of dumb shit to complain about, for sure. But owning this place, in itself an advantage, has afforded freedoms that I've chosen, at times, to ignore in favor of feeling put-upon. Freedoms like not worrying too much about where the mortgage payment is coming from; like having a little left over to travel, eat good food, drink nice wine, take care of myself; like the luxury of growing my own food, which should not be a luxury; like having my own permanent place to live, a place I can count on as long as I need it. And—most importantly—like *being the landlady* instead of getting played by some scammer landlord.

When I squint through the keyhole into a possible future life, just Dave and Runi and me in our own diminutive house, I conjure up a sense of ease. It might be a less demanding life. It might be peaceful: a fireplace, another dog, Miles Davis on the stereo, banana bread in the oven and soup on the stove. Just as brightly, though, I get a flash of it—shit, I would miss Penn Street! I would miss the noise, the 24/7 racket of people going out, coming in, swapping parking spots. I would miss the weirdos who live with me. I would miss being available at all hours, being the one in charge of the solution when there is a problem. I would miss hearing parties going on below my feet. I would miss saying hello to a variety of cats in the hallway. I would miss my garden, my refuge, which I could imitate but never duplicate elsewhere. I would miss the hoppy sweetness of weed smoke filtering through my floorboards. I would miss the bits of outside conversations that drift up to my apartment on the wind. I would miss the dingy, warped floors, the misaligned corners, the myriad of half-busted things competing for my money and attention. I would miss the adversity.

Having been moderately lucky in the parts of life that really matter, I've had to manufacture my own adversity, my own losing battle; PennHenge is the inexhaustible well of hardship of my subconscious desires. I don't believe that taking it easy is a place of comfort for me.

From the beginning, the endeavor of my home-ownership has been based in blind determination, a sense that if I keep rushing forward, someday I'll not feel like an amateur. But why wouldn't I feel like one? The notion has been reinforced over these last twelve years by realtors, electricians, plumbers, tax collectors, tenants, cops—male and female—who treated me like I had no shot in this game by dint of my being a young, physically unimposing woman. As if an atypical player could never find a way to win the game. I used to resent such assumptions, but now my experience speaks for itself. I don't need to justify what I've done here to anyone. Besides, how would "winning" be defined in my case? I would say it's keeping the house in decent repair, being a good neighbor, and providing a modest but safe place to live for six to ten people at a time. Others would judge it financially and tell me I should be exacting the maximum number of dollars from the house, no matter how shady the required deeds might seem. I've had contractors suggest I finish part of the basement and illegally rent it out, for example; other landlords tell me I should be raising the rent every year, no matter what, just to keep my tenants on their toes.

I've not taken the most direct route toward success in landladyhood—by any definition—but I can say that I've been an honest, extremely fallible human woman: a wimp, a badass, a fool, a queen, and a dipshit. And I hereby claim my right to keep occupying all of those roles.

How else could I do this thing?

I never wanted a dream home. I wanted a struggle, and I got one. All these years on, I still have trouble imagining a household that doesn't max out my mental and financial resources. I've proven to myself and anyone else who's expressed doubt that I can endure it all, and do it with a smile and a shrug.

PennHenge, you taught me how.

You're my ruthless muse, and I adore you.

You've forced me to make uncomfortable decisions in search of sweet equilibrium—not just when to change the drapes, but whether to call the cops; leave an inert relationship; stand up to a total asshole; or fight for what I want. In so doing, you've shaped me into an adult. Maybe that adult is not, when it comes down to it, all that well suited to being a landlady; maybe I'm too sensitive, too lenient, too wary of money, too comfortable avoiding confrontation. The lessons from you have come rapidly, like punches hitting me squarely between the eyes, but they're nothing to regret. You've never let me squirm out from under my responsibilities, though my urge is often to do just that. Every one of your problems is my problem in the end, and caring for you, my disobedient charge, is a thorny delight.

Acknowledgments

I would like to thank my agent, Cheryl Pientka at Jill Grinberg Literary Management, whose enthusiasm for this project—even as a wisp of an idea—gave me the push to make it real. Also to Sarah Weston, for her instrumental comments and suggestions.

Thank you to the good people at the Feminist Press, including Jamia Wilson, Suki Boynton, Drew Stevens, Jisu Kim, Hannah Goodwin, Lucia Brown, Lauren Hook, and Sophia Magnone. To Jennifer Baumgardner, who saw the value in my story, worked with me to find the parts of it that needed telling, and helped me to muster the might to get them on the page. And to Alyea Canada, who lovingly helped me carry the book through to the finish.

Heather Toupin, Elana Wetzner, Dan Boucher, Steven Lloyd, Cassie Tharinger, Liz Lee, Julie Shore, Jacob Berendes, Kate Schapira, Jori Ketten, Tom Roach, Deb Wood, Chrissy Wolpert, Seth Manchester, Mandy McCorkle, Anja Lademann, James Quigley, Brian Simmons, Hilary Treadwell, Bernadette Baker-Baughman, Karen Pace, Frank and Cathy Lifrieri: thank you for offering support, curiosity, and ideas during this process.

To Nick Gomez-Hall, who left the world during the writing of this book: your light will inspire me always.

Thank you to 186 Carpenter, the Providence Athenaeum, and the Providence Public Library for giving me places to work that are not my kitchen table.

Thank you to all the human beings who have lived at PennHenge during my time. The house and I have our failings, but I hope (most of) you would agree it's not a bad place to make your bed. You have never sought to curb my expression of the experience for this book. Years from now, I'll still be thinking of ways in which you made me better, stronger.

All the landladies everywhere, and especially my Providence crew, who have helped me get by: Adrienne, Sarah, Cynthia, Reba, SueEllen.

To my plumber, Anne Flores, who does her job with integrity and care; thank you.

RIP Buster, feline guru of PennHenge.

To my dog Runi: you are the best partner for neighborhood explorations.

And thanks to my husband, Dave, whose footfalls to the third floor are the most welcome of sounds.

The Feminist Press is a nonprofit educational organization founded to amplify feminist voices. FP publishes classic and new writing from around the world, creates cutting-edge programs, and elevates silenced and marginalized voices in order to support personal transformation and social justice for all people.

See our complete list of books at
feministpress.org